Plain

Speaking

How to Preach and Teach

Effectively

David Bercot

SCROLL

PUBLISHING

Published by Scroll Publishing Company, P. O. Box 122, Amberson, PA 17210.

(717) 349-7033

ISBN: 978-0-924722-18-9

Printed in the United States of America.

Cover photograph © Scroll Publishing Co.

Contents

Various Aspects of Preaching

1

It Doesn't Take a Seminary Education to Preach Well

I still remember the first time I got up to speak in front of a church. It was only a five-minute message, but my heart was pounding as I approached the podium. My hands literally trembled, and I was sure I would forget my opening statements. My voice seemed unnaturally high when I began to speak, and I mispronounced words that I normally have no trouble saying. I even got tongue-tied several times. Naturally, I couldn't wait to get back to my seat.

Actually, my experience was normal for first-time speakers. According to the *Book of Lists*, Americans rank fear of speaking in public as their number one fear. They actually fear it more than death (which was rated number seven).[1]

But preaching (or any other form of public speaking) does not have to be something to fear. It can and *should* be something to anticipate. Today, I enjoy preaching, rather than dreading it. What's more, I'm totally confident this can become your experience as well.

Why Another Book on Public Speaking?

There have been literally hundreds of books written on public speaking and preaching. So why am I writing another one? Well, it's not because I know some secrets about preaching that no one else knows. The basic principles we'll be looking at in this book are the same principles covered by virtually every other book on public speaking.

However, most books written about preaching are addressed to salaried, seminary-trained pastors. They're not aimed at churches that don't use seminary-trained ministers. Nor are they aimed at churches that use ordinary members of the congregation to give short devotional messages. So that's why I'm writing this book.

I'm writing specifically to you men who have no seminary training. You may be an ordained minister who preaches on a regular basis. Or you may be a brother who occasionally teaches Sunday School or presents a ten-minute devotional once every few months. Either way, you have no seminary education. Is there anything wrong with that? Of course not. The New Testament Christians had no seminaries, but they raised up effective preachers and teachers. I firmly believe that the Holy Spirit can use ordinary Christian men today to preach and teach—just as He did back in the first century.

I should mention at the outset that when I use the terms "preaching" and "teaching" in this book, I'm using the terms interchangeably. And, as I've indicated, I'm not referring to Sunday morning sermons alone, but also to ten-minute devotional messages and Sunday school lessons. It's just as important to preach effectively in these shorter messages as it is in the main sermon.

I myself attend a church that has no seminary-trained ministers. And I firmly believe that the quality of preaching in churches like ours should not be one bit inferior to that of conventional churches with professionally trained ministers. If anything, it should be better.

However, I also know that too often this isn't the case. In churches like ours, I've heard many excellent sermons and devotionals. But, I've also heard many rambling messages with no clear theme or goal, delivered in an unenthusiastic, monotone voice.

My desire is to see *every* sermon and devotional preached in our churches be an effective message that blesses our listeners. More importantly, *God* wants to see that. And it's not an unattainable goal. Only three things are needed:

- The anointing of the Holy Spirit

- The *desire* to learn to preach

- Some basic training in how to prepare and deliver an effective message.

Jesus commanded His followers, "Whatever I tell you in the dark, speak in the light; and what you hear in the ear, preach on the housetops" (Matt. 10:27). Jesus would not have commanded His followers to preach the gospel unless He was going to give them the power to preach effectively. The power is there for all Spirit-begotten Christian men who earnestly seek it. You just have to step out in faith.

You also must have a burning desire to preach well. Without the desire to be an effective speaker, all the training in the world will do little good.

---

[1]David Wallechinsky, et al, *The Book of Lists* (Denver, William Morrow & Co., 1977), p. 4.

Discussion Questions

1. According to the *Book of Lists*, what do the majority of Americans fear the most?

2. Why is a seminary education not necessary for a person to become an effective speaker?

3. What are the three things needed to preach effectively?

2

Don't Settle for Mediocrity

The one thing that will determine whether you become an excellent speaker or not is your *desire*. As one writer put it, "If I could measure your desire, I could determine almost exactly your success as a speaker."[1] There is no such thing as a born speaker. The men who excel in preaching all had the desire to be effective preachers. And that desire counted more than any natural talents they may have possessed at birth. Those men refused to settle for mediocrity.

I attend a conservative Anabaptist church. The Anabaptist spiritual family includes the Mennonite, Amish, and Brethren churches. One thing I've observed is that the men in our churches rarely settle for mediocrity when it comes to their secular trades. For example, a Mennonite carpenter usually is known for the high quality of his work. Likewise, people travel hundreds of miles to purchase Amish-crafted furniture.

In our Anabaptist circles, most of us would *never* sell one of our customers a hastily prepared, haphazardly assembled piece of furniture. We take pride in the quality of our craftsmanship. If we don't settle for mediocrity in our trades, how much more so should we not accept it in our preaching and teaching.

"We are ambassadors for Christ," Paul tells us (2 Cor. 5:20). What an incredible privilege! Christ does not *have to* use frail humans as His ambassadors. He could use mighty angels instead. And they would be glad to serve in that capacity. In fact, I'm sure they would make wonderful ambassadors. But, no, God chose to deny the angels that privilege and to give it to us instead. What a wonderful Lord He is!

Why We Should Have the Desire

When we speak in front of a congregation, we're not representing ourselves. We're representing Christ. We're speaking as ambassadors of His kingdom. We have the opportunity to speak as Christ's personal representatives about the matters that are important to Him.

I can honestly say that I thoroughly enjoy preaching and teaching—speaking as an ambassador of Christ. To be sure, scheduling the necessary time for preparation isn't always easy. And, like most other speakers, I experience speaker's fright before I preach. But as soon as I get past my first sentence, it is an experience I cherish. In fact, I always feel a tinge of excitement when our pastor asks me to speak on a future Sunday.

There is something really special about being able to speak about God, His Word, and the Christian life. It is indeed a privilege. But it's also a responsibility.

Our Responsibility as Brothers

Paul told Timothy, "I do not permit a woman to teach or to have authority over a man" (1 Tim. 2:12). For this reason, in Bible-believing churches, men do all the preaching. This is a wonderful privilege God has given us men. But God's privileges always come with responsibilities. It's hardly fair to the sisters for us men to do all the preaching—and then do a shoddy job of it. If God will not allow sisters to preach in church, then they are at least entitled to hear quality sermons and devotionals from their brothers. Not just occasionally, but *all* of the time.

Under the Mosaic Law, men were given many special privileges that God did not extend to the women. But God also laid some heavy responsibilities on the men, from which He exempted the women. For instance, the men had to fight all the wars. Many of them never came back alive from their battles. During the period of the Judges, every Israelite man was a soldier whether he wanted to be one or not (unless he was a Levite). It was his responsibility.

If an Israelite man wanted to live through the next battle and to effectively protect his family and nation, he had to practice his fighting skills. If he went to battle not knowing how to use a sword or throw a spear, he was placing his own life at great risk. He also was failing in his responsibility to his family and nation. Yet, those Israelite men during the time of the Judges were not *professional* soldiers. Nobody paid them to go to war. They had to train on their own time.

Today, the type of battle we men fight for the Lord is of a different kind. As Paul said, "The weapons of our warfare are not carnal." We don't use swords or guns in our battles, but *words*. Paul said our responsibility is to be "pulling down strongholds, casting down arguments and every high thing that exalts itself against the knowledge of God" (2 Cor. 10:4,5). If we are to be effective soldiers for God, we *must* learn to speak effectively.

Your Message Can Change Lives

A speaker never knows for sure what impact his message may have on lives. However, the potential is great. There may be first-time visitors to your church on the Sunday when you speak. They may be seeking to join a church where the Bible is taught without its message being watered down. This may be their first time to visit a church like yours. They probably will form a lasting impression of your church based largely on your sermon or devotional.

Or, through your message, you might convict someone about unrepented sin in his life. Or perhaps you'll lead someone to surrender his life to Christ. Maybe you'll bring out an important Biblical truth that your hearers had never known before. Or perhaps you'll provide badly needed encouragement to those who are downhearted. The potential is enormous.

Most Christians spend the larger part of the week in providing and caring for their families. They need to be spiritually recharged and nourished on Sundays and Wednesday nights. We brothers dare not waste that precious, limited time. We can't afford to present some disorganized, rambling discourse that neither feeds nor revitalizes anyone.

Reliance on the Holy Spirit

This book primarily focuses on the *practical* aspects of preaching and teaching. But it's important that you understand that the practical steps to becoming an effective speaker are secondary to the work of the Holy Spirit in your life as a Christian and as a speaker. You can master the practical aspects of public speaking, but without the power of God, you won't be an effective preacher.

Furthermore, you'll probably find that without the empowerment from God, you won't even make much progress on the practical elements of preaching. So I encourage you to make preaching a constant subject of heartfelt prayer. Fall on your face before God and implore Him to enable you to master each of the basic components of preaching we'll be talking about.

The early Anabaptists lit a fire in sixteenth-century Europe that nobody was able to put out. One of the secrets of their effectiveness was their total dependence on the Holy Spirit. The Spirit imbued them with such power that hearts melted when they preached, and thousands flocked to their spiritual movement. Plain preaching today should be no different. The same Holy Spirit is still present, and He will empower us to preach just as effectively if we will surrender ourselves to Him and earnestly entreat Him.

Is It "Unspiritual" to Train?

Some Christians have the notion that it is somehow "unspiritual" to train as preachers and teachers. They imagine that reliance on the Holy Spirit means we don't need any further training to become effective preachers.

But was that the approach Jesus took? Not at all. He selected his twelve apostles near the beginning of His ministry and personally taught and trained them for years before He turned the leadership of the church over to them. He sent them out on preaching trips so that they could gain experience. He gave them lengthy, specific instructions when He sent them out, and He received their feedback when they returned (Matt. 10). His apostles had *both* the anointing of the Holy Spirit and the needed training.

Joshua trained under Moses. Elisha trained under Elijah. Timothy and Titus trained under Paul. Paul directed Timothy to train men who would eventually take Timothy's place: "The things that you have heard from me among many witnesses, commit these to faithful men who will be *able to teach others* also" (2 Tim. 2:2).

Although the Anabaptist movement was primarily a movement of the Holy Spirit, many of the early Anabaptist preachers had training in rhetoric (the art of persuasion through public speaking and writing). I'm speaking of such early Anabaptist leaders as Conrad Grebel, Felix Manz, George Blaurock, and Pilgram Marpeck. The training of these men in speaking and writing only enhanced the work the Holy Spirit did through them.

Dependence on God does not mean that we Christians do nothing ourselves. We depend upon God for our food and sustenance. But that doesn't mean we don't have to work for our needs. Nor does it mean that we refuse to receive training in our various trades. Likewise, dependence on the Holy Spirit for our preaching doesn't negate the need for training.

It's similar to David's combat with Goliath. David was a man of valor who was mighty in the Spirit of God. When he went out in faith to fight Goliath, he was depending upon the power of God, not his own strength. Yet, he didn't just rush out to confront Goliath unarmed, hoping maybe that God would strike Goliath dead with a lightning bolt or something. Rather, he armed himself with a sling, a weapon that he had mastered through years of practice.

As soldiers of God, we are often confronted with the giants of our age. We must depend upon the power of the Spirit to vanquish these giants. But like David, we should never fight the enemy unarmed. One of our primary weapons is our preaching. Let's be sure that we master this weapon as well as David mastered the use of his sling.

_____

[1]Ronald L. Willingham, *How to Speak So People Will Listen* (Waco, Word Books, 1968), p. 13.

Discussion Questions

1. What is one of the primary things that will determine whether or not a person will become an excellent speaker?

2. Why should we have the desire to learn to speak effectively?

3. What responsibility has God given to the men in the church?

4. What potential impact can your sermon have on others?

5. What key role does the Holy Spirit play in our preaching?

6. Why is it not "unspiritual" to receive training in speaking?

3

Anyone Can Learn To Speak Effectively

For most of your life, you may have thought that only certain men with special gifts are able to preach and teach well. But it's not that way at all. Virtually *anyone* can learn to speak effectively in public. Really! If you're a Spirit-begotten Christian man and are capable of carrying on a conversation, then you're capable of preaching and teaching. That's because good preaching is simply a form of structured conversation.

No man was ever *born* as a superb craftsman or tradesman. He not only had to have the desire, but he also had to receive adequate training. It's the same way with preaching. The Spirit wants to use you and will give you the enabling power. But you have to be willing to learn.

Learning to preach is like learning to sing. For most of my life, I thought only a few select people had the gift of singing. And definitely I wasn't one of those select few! So in church, I fumbled through hymns, trying to hit the notes as best I could. Yet I was invariably off key, and the only time I sang with much volume was when I was around others who sang loudly and would drown out my own feeble attempts.

However, when I began attending an Anabaptist church, I slowly came to realize that almost *everyone* can learn to sing. All it takes is a bit of training. Mennonite and Amish schools typically teach singing as a part of their curriculum. That's why their people sing so well. By the time they've reached high school age, most Mennonite youths not only can sing well, but they also can sing various parts—such as bass, tenor, and alto.

Public speaking is no different. Capable speakers are made, not born. All it takes is God's power, your desire, and proper training. And that's the purpose of this book—to teach you *how* to speak. If I hadn't received training in my youth in preaching, I would never be able to preach effectively today.

I can assure you that public speaking doesn't come naturally to me. Nor am I the most accomplished speaker you'll ever hear. I'm simply a fellow brother in Christ with ordinary preaching skills. But I can present an organized, clear message, and I can hold a congregation's attention for an hour. That's what I want to teach you to be able to do.

Discussion Questions

1. Good preaching is a form of what?
2. What parallel is there between learning to sing and learning to preach?

4

Preaching Is Organized Conversation

Please understand that I'm not going to be teaching you how to "make a speech." You need to clear everything out of your head that you've ever been taught about "making speeches." What I'm going to teach you is how to have a *conversation* with a congregation. Making speeches is for politicians. When you preach or teach, you want to converse with your brothers and sisters.

Of course, you already know how to converse with people. In fact, more than likely, you're a much better conversationalist than I am. I have enormous difficulty starting up a conversation with others. No doubt, you have a huge head start over me. So if *I* have been able to learn to preach and teach, *you* definitely can learn to do so.

Imagine that you've just returned from a missionary visit to Central America. After the Sunday service, you're standing near the front of the church telling two or three friends about your trip. You don't need anyone to teach you how to do that, do you? It's an ability you were born with. As you speak to your friends, you're not the least bit nervous. You're not fumbling for words or wondering what you're going to say next. Without even thinking about it, you tell about your trip in a way that's interesting and that follows some sort of logical sequence. Your friends enjoy what you're sharing with them, and you don't have to worry about holding their interest.

Imagine that after a few minutes, a few more friends come over to listen. Now you have five or six listeners instead of two or three. Does that change anything? Of course not. You'll simply continue on as you had been doing. After awhile, four or five others join the group of listeners. Should that change anything? No, talking to ten or twelve people isn't any different from talking to two or three. You'll probably speak a bit louder, but that's all.

Now, let's further imagine that more and more brothers and sisters come over to listen to you. Eventually you have an audience of forty or fifty people. Should that cause you to suddenly change your manner of speaking? Does your conversation suddenly have to turn into a "speech"? Do you now have to become stiff and formal in the way you talk? Of course not! There's really no reason why anything has to change.

You instinctively know how to speak when you're conversing with others. You realize how to make it interesting—how to hold your hearers' attention—without even thinking about it. The good news is that preaching is simply organized conversation. If you can converse with others, you can preach. As a result, you already know much of what there is to learn about preaching. The biggest difficulty you may face is having to *unlearn* a lot of notions you've grown up with.

How Preaching Differs from Conversation

Although good preaching is simply a form of structured conversation, there are some important differences between preaching and *everyday* conversations.

The first difference, of course, is dependence on the Holy Spirit. You don't normally pray before you begin a conversation with someone, but you should never begin work on a sermon without earnest prayer and a deep sense of dependence on God for His guidance.

A second difference is that normal conversation requires no preparation. Most people probably don't even know *what* they're going to talk about when they begin talking. Instead, the conversation develops on its own. It may concern some deep truths or issues, or it may be rather trivial. Often the purpose of everyday conversation is merely to enjoy the company of our friends and to share life's experiences with each other. It doesn't need to have any other goal.

But that will never do for preaching and teaching. Your preaching *must* have a point to it, and this *will* require thorough preparation. When you preach, you're not there to entertain the congregation or merely to pass some time in each other's company. You're there for a specific purpose: to encourage, to exhort, to convict, or to pass on important spiritual truths. You have a vital message you want to get across to your hearers.

Another difference is that in ordinary conversation, it's not natural for one person to be doing all the talking for an extended period. What keeps conversation interesting is the interchange between speakers. But in preaching, only one person is doing the talking. It takes some training to be able to do that effectively. That part of preaching doesn't come naturally for most people. It certainly didn't for me.

Training in effective speaking can be divided into two basic areas: preparation and delivery. What listeners observe is your delivery. But what makes that delivery effective is your *preparation*. If there is one secret to preaching effectively, it is this: thorough preparation.

Is Preparation Really Needed?

Just as some Christians imagine that training in speaking is unnecessary, others have the notion that we shouldn't prepare our sermons in advance. Rather, we should just let the Holy Spirit direct us once we reach the podium. But where do the Scriptures say that?

The only passage that remotely comes to mind is Mark 13:11, where Jesus said: "When they arrest you and deliver you up, do not worry beforehand, or premeditate what you will speak. But whatever is given you in that hour, speak that; for it is not you who speak, but the Holy Spirit." Now, did Jesus say we shouldn't prepare beforehand when we preach and teach in our *congregations*? No, He did not. He limited His command to the times when we are arrested and brought before government authorities.

Instead of telling us not to prepare our sermons ahead of time, the implication of Jesus' command in Mark 13:11 is just the opposite. The fact that He tells us not to prepare in that one particular situation implies that we *should* prepare in other situations.

As one speaker has put it: "Following a systematic method for constructing a sermon does not rule out nor does it limit the guidance of the Holy Spirit. Orderliness, not confusion, is the evidence of the leading of the Holy Spirit."[1] When I read the Scriptures, I see a God of preparation. He carefully prepared the earth for man's habitation. He had Noah make extensive preparations for the Flood. He spent thousands of years preparing mankind for the coming of His Son. And He even sent out John the Baptist beforehand to "prepare the way of the Lord" (Matt. 3:3). Organization and preparation are earmarks of God's handiwork.

If the Spirit can guide you when you are in the pulpit, He can just as easily guide you at your desk when you're contemplating what to preach. Why place limits on where the Spirit can work and where He can't? Famous preachers through the centuries, such as John Wesley, have all carefully prepared their messages.

If you think the Spirit can work better without your preparation, why not get some candid feedback from your listeners? What do *they* have to say? Why not record and play back one of your unprepared sermons and compare it with a recorded sermon from someone who thoroughly prepared ahead of time. Which one is more effective? Which one has the Spirit blessed? Are people drawn to your church because of the excellent preaching there?

I firmly believe that God wants and expects us to prepare our messages ahead of time. That's because He desires the very best from us. So now let's talk a few minutes about *how* to prepare.

---

[1]Lloyd M. Perry, *Biblical Preaching for Today's World* (Chicago, Moody Press, 1973), p. 44.

Discussion Questions

1. Will this book teach someone how to "make a speech"?

2. How does preaching differ from ordinary conversation?

3. Training in public speaking can be divided into what two basic areas?

4. Is it Scripturally wrong to prepare sermons ahead of time?

5

Preparing Seven Days a Week

If you wait until the night before you speak and then begin preparing your message, you've already lost the battle. Unless you're blessed with a quick mind and a glib tongue, your sermon will probably never rise above mediocrity. You're cheating your brothers and sisters—and more importantly, your Lord.

Preparation for preaching and teaching has to be something you do twenty-four hours a day, seven days a week. It's not something you do on Saturday night. It has to be a way of life. I don't say that just to the brothers in ordained ministry, but to all of us who preach and teach in any capacity.

Now, when I speak of "preparing seven days a week," I'm not meaning that you're going to be working on your sermon outline seven days a week. Rather, I mean that on a daily basis you must view life and its varied experiences as a wealth of material to use in teaching others about God and His kingdom.

For a Christian, every day is filled with blessings, tests, triumphs, trials, and life experiences. These become a storehouse for someone who preaches. As one writer put it, "The man who is continually living under the influence and power of the Holy Spirit will scarcely ever be at a loss for something to preach about."[1] And again, "Let the Christian life master and take complete possession of him—then let him preach about it."[2]

Perhaps you're an auto mechanic by trade. But regardless of your trade, your real profession is being an ambassador of Christ. So in your daily experiences with engines and your interactions with customers, you need to consider what lessons you can learn about the Christian life and the kingdom of God. Perhaps you're working on a sluggish engine and you discover that the problem is a clogged fuel filter. The car has plenty of gas, but the gas is not fully reaching the engine because the grime in the fuel filter is blocking it. As an ambassador of Christ, you might see the similarity with sin. Sin in our lives can block the flow of the Holy Spirit into our souls, choking out spiritual growth and power.

Reflect on Your Experiences

At the end of each day, reflect on that day's experiences and on the conversations you've had with various people. Are there lessons there to be learned? Did something happen that would make good material to be included in a sermon? Reflect on what you've learned from the day's experiences and on what God may have been trying to teach you through them.

On most days, you probably won't recognize anything of particular significance to be used in a message. But if you make it a practice to look at the events of each day through the eyes of a preacher, you *will* find lessons and analogies from time to time—and possible sermon topics.

Be An Observer

Of course, if you go through life with your eyes half closed, you won't have anything on which to reflect at the end of the day. Jesus was a keen observer, and that's one reason He was such a superb teacher. Notice His many references to everyday life:

"When you do a charitable deed, do not sound a trumpet before you as the hypocrites do in the synagogues and in the streets" (Matt. 6:2).

"When you pray, do not use vain repetitions as the heathen do" (Matt. 6:7).

"Consider the lilies of the field, how they grow: they neither toil nor spin; and yet I say to you that even Solomon in all his glory was not arrayed like one of these" (Matt. 6:28,29).

"Nor do they put new wine into old wineskins, or else the wineskins break" (Matt. 9:17).

"What man is there among you who has one sheep, and if it falls into a pit on the Sabbath, will not lay hold of it and lift it out?" (Matt. 12:11).

"The kingdom of heaven is like a merchant seeking beautiful pearls, who, when he had found one pearl of great price, went and sold all that he had and bought it" (Matt. 13:45,46).

"When it is evening you say, 'It will be fair weather, for the sky is red'; and in the morning, 'It will be foul weather today, for the sky is red and threatening'" (Matt. 16:2,3).

The list could go on and on. The point is that Jesus was a keen observer of life—of both the good things and the bad, of both major events and seemingly trivial ones. However, most of us aren't born observers. It's an art we have to cultivate. I encourage you to begin practicing this art, for it will have an enormous impact on your preaching.

Safeguard Your Treasures

Unfortunately, it won't do you much good to reflect on the events of each day unless you *preserve* in writing the lessons, illustrations, and sermon topics that come to your mind. I keep a file of ideas and illustrations for sermons and books. If I did not keep a written file, I'm sure I would quickly forget these ideas. So if you're serious about becoming an effective speaker, I encourage you too to keep some sort of written notebook or file of your reflections and thoughts for sermons. Label and organize these reflections well, so that you can quickly find them later.

I find that some of my best illustrations and sermon topics come when I'm lying in bed with the lights out. I can finally clear my mind of the day's problems and responsibilities. I don't *try* to think about sermon topics. In fact, I attempt to do just the opposite: I try to blank everything out of my mind, so I can fall asleep. But, then, somehow things pop into my mind. Sometimes I suddenly get an exciting idea for a sermon topic—or, perhaps an illustration for a sermon. I think perhaps God finds that an ideal time to speak to me.

I realize that if I fall asleep I probably won't remember these insights when I wake up. But I really don't want to get out of bed, creep to the kitchen in the dark, and find a pen and some paper. So what I've finally learned is to keep a legal pad and a pen on the night table next to my bed. When an idea flashes into my mind at night, I simply lean over, grab the legal pad and pen, and jot down the idea. Even though I write in the dark, I've always been able to decipher my scribbling in the morning. The next day, I re-write the idea in better handwriting and file it away. A lot of the thoughts shared in this book came to me that way.

Referring to the need to prepare seven days a week, one preacher said: "The preacher's main business is not to preach sermons; it is to gather and proclaim truth. Therefore the preacher's whole life should be spent in seeking for truth for truth's sake and not for the mere sake of sermon preparation. He must learn to gather his material before he undertakes the preparation of his sermon. During the process of building, does a builder quarry the needed stones by putting one stone into place and then going away to quarry, cut and shape another, and so on? No; he sees to it that the material he needs is on the ground before the building is commenced."[3]

Be a Constant Reader

A good speaker must be a good reader. Jesus said, "Out of the abundance of the heart, the mouth speaks" (Matt. 12:34). If you don't have an abundance inside, you won't have much to say to a congregation when it comes time to preach. One of the ways that you can build up an inner storehouse of knowledge and spirituality is through reading.

For ambassadors of Christ, there is no substitute for daily Bible reading. At a minimum, you should read through the entire New Testament at least once a year. Many Christians make it their goal to read through both Testaments annually. If you want to be an effective teacher, you need to be thoroughly familiar with the Bible. You shouldn't have to look up in a reference book what the Bible says on most doctrinal and moral issues. You should already know.

Daily Bible reading not only nourishes your soul, but it also provides you with potential sermon topics. Even though I've read through the Bible countless times, I never cease to be amazed that I discover new things virtually every time I read it. I know of no other book like that. I don't mean that I discover new doctrines or commandments. Rather, I uncover new insights and perspectives on familiar doctrines and commandments. I also discover new lessons from the lives of the men and women of the Bible.

You should supplement your Bible reading with other books: daily devotionals, biographies of outstanding Christians, quality Christian periodicals, and books on Christian living. These all can nourish us and provide insights and topics for preaching. I've been especially blessed by the writings of early Christians such as Justin Martyr and Tertullian and by classic Christian works through the centuries. Two of my favorite Christian classics are *A Serious Call to a Devout and Holy Life* and *The Imitation of Christ.*

One writer has said: "To be prolific in thought one must be a faithful reader. . . .The constant reader will not be at a loss for thoughts. The man who does not read much will not make much of a preacher."[4]

Again, as with your daily experiences, you need to write down insights you gain from your reading. If you don't write them down and file them away, you're likely to forget them and will never be able to share them with others.

"But I Preach Only Twice a Year"

If you preach on a regular basis, this type of daily preparation is essential if you're going to consistently deliver stimulating, meaningful sermons. But you may be thinking to yourself, "Yes, but all I ever do is to deliver a ten-minute devotional message about once every six months. So surely I don't need that type of ongoing preparation." But you do.

Even if it's only for ten minutes twice a year, you need to make the most of those ten-minute messages. If all our brothers who deliver short devotionals prepared seven days a week, think of how their insightful devotionals would bless our churches! Those devotional messages would be the high point of every service because so much thought had gone into them.

"But I'm Too Busy"

You may be thinking to yourself, "But, David, I'm too busy to devote that much time to preparing a sermon or devotional message. I have a large family to support, and it leaves me little free time." I have a very full schedule myself, so I can well relate to what you're saying. But we're the very ones who *must* work on our messages seven days a week, fifty-two weeks a year. Such preparation not only enables us to have more effective sermons, but it also saves enormous amounts of time.

I don't have to spend hours and hours at my desk trying to think of what to preach about, how to develop my sermons, and ways to illustrate them. Instead, I'm doing all of those things while I'm driving, brushing my teeth, and mowing the lawn.

What Steps Are Needed For Preparation?

"But what sort of preparation is needed for a sermon or devotional?" you may be wondering. There are a number of things you need to do in preparing for a sermon. We'll cover them one by one. The first step is to choose the right topic.

---

[1]William Evans, *How to Prepare Sermons* (Chicago: Moody Press, 1964), p. 27.

[2]*Ibid.* p. 44

[3]*Ibid.* p. 56

[4]*Ibid.* p. 50.

Discussion Questions

1. How many days a week should we be preparing our messages?

2. At the end of each day, what type of reflection should we do?

3. Give examples that demonstrate that Jesus was a keen observer.

4. How can a person preserve his observations and reflections?

5. Why is reading important to becoming a good speaker?

6. What if we feel we're too busy to prepare seven days a week?

Exercises

a. **Instructor**: Have the students reflect on various observations or experiences in their lives over the past few weeks. Have them orally share at least one spiritual illustration based on one of these experiences or observations.

b. **Instructor**: Have the students discuss any new insights they have had from their Bible reading over the past few months or from any spiritual classics they have recently read.

6

Choosing the Right Topic

The topic you choose will often make or break your sermon. If you choose the wrong topic, the results almost certainly will be unsatisfactory—no matter how much time you spend in preparation. But what is the *right* topic? To be "right," a topic has to be

- Right for *you*
- Right for the congregation to which you're speaking
- Right for the time allotted for your message.

The first step is to pray earnestly about the topic of your message. You want God to help you choose the topic that will be right for the situation at hand. Never just casually choose a sermon topic as you would the subject for a school essay.

Right for *You*

To be right for *you*, a topic has to be one that captures your interest. If you're not interested in the topic, you're going to have a hard time interesting your audience in it. You also need to strongly believe in your topic. If you don't passionately and earnestly believe what you're going to be preaching, your message is likely to be dull and wishy-washy.

For a topic to be right for you, you need to know a lot about it. You should thoroughly grasp your topic through years of experience or because you have carefully researched it. In other words, you need to master your subject before you speak about it. Once you do, you'll be able to speak confidently and authoritatively.

Right for the Congregation

At the same time, you're not preaching for your own edification. Your message is for the benefit of the congregation. So your subject should also be appropriate for the congregation to whom you're speaking. It would make little sense to preach against speeding on the roads if you're addressing a congregation of Old Order Amish. Hundreds of topics fascinate me personally, but many of them would probably not interest my listeners.

Your message also should be one that your listeners *need* to hear. It should be tailored to their situation and spiritual needs. If your sermon is going to be primarily informative, then it needs to impart information that your listeners don't already know. Yet, it shouldn't be so far above their heads that they can't follow your presentation.

Likewise, if you will be discussing a particular sin or spiritual weakness, it should be one that is common to your hearers. Don't talk about sins that are common at the First Presbyterian church in town if you're preaching at Green Meadow Mennonite Church. If God is going to be able to speak through you as you preach, you need to be addressing sins or weaknesses that are common to your listeners.

Right for the Allotted Time

A topic is not "right" if you can't adequately cover it in the time allotted to you. If you're going to be delivering a ten-minute devotional, you don't want to choose as your topic the "Basic Doctrines of Christianity" or the "Life of Moses." Nor do you want to try to deliver an expository message on an entire chapter of the Bible. Focus on one fairly narrow topic or on a few select verses with a common theme.

On the other hand, if you're delivering a one-hour sermon, you'll want to choose a subject that will require a full hour for proper development. Few things are more tedious than listening for an hour to a speaker who chose a topic he can cover adequately in twenty minutes. After twenty minutes, he has said all he can say on the topic. At that point, he should just sit down. But because the congregation expects an hour-long sermon, he instead spends forty wearisome minutes just rehashing what he has already said.

Often you won't know in advance if your topic will fit the allotted time. You won't know until you begin preparing your outline. With experience, you should soon learn how to predict how long a message will take based on the number of outline pages. For example, I have found that with my initial detailed outlines, eight pages equals about sixty minutes of speaking time. As you're preparing, if you see that your message is going to be either too long or too short, you need to take care of the matter right there and then. Don't wait until you're in front of the congregation and hopelessly over or under the allotted time.

If the problem is that you have too much material, try narrowing your topic. For example, if your original subject was "Lessons from the Lives of the Patriarchs," you might want to change it to "Lessons from the Life of Abraham." Any material you've prepared on the other patriarchs can be used in future sermons.

Having too broad a topic is easier to fix than having one that's too narrow. If you can't come up with enough material for your topic, you may need to broaden it. Returning to our example, let's suppose that your topic was originally "Lessons from the Life of Abraham." However, you just cannot come up with enough material to fill out a sermon. The answer might be to broaden the topic to "Lessons from the Lives of Abraham and Isaac" or "Lessons from the Lives of the Patriarchs."

Nevertheless, you'll have trouble expanding some topics. In those situations, you'll have to bite the bullet and accept the fact that your topic just isn't going to work. You need to choose a different topic.

That's why you don't want to wait until Saturday night to prepare your message. If it's nine o'clock Saturday night, and you've just spent an hour working on your message, you're going to be reluctant to abandon it and start over. What's the result? The likely result is that the next morning you'll probably end up forcing your listeners to hear a twenty-minute sermon that's been stretched to sixty minutes by means of tedious repetition and incoherent rambling.

When to Choose Your Topic

At the church I attend, our pastor usually notifies us of speaking assignments about a month in advance—which is certainly adequate notice. But I don't wait until he notifies me. Rather, I start thinking and praying about a topic for my next sermon immediately after I finish preaching my present one. That gives me lots of time to choose a topic, to ponder how to develop that topic, and to think of illustrations and examples. It also means that I have plenty of time to discard the topic and choose another one if I see that it just won't work.

In the previous chapter, I talked about preparing seven days a week. Such preparation becomes much more meaningful if you already have a sermon subject in mind. It will enable you to relate events and conversations to a particular topic. Without even spending any extra time out of your busy day, you may find that many of the illustrations and developmental points of your sermon will come to you throughout the course of daily life. Again, that's why you want to choose your topic as far in advance as possible.

But it's not enough simply to have a good topic for your sermon. You also must have a *goal*.

Discussion Questions

1. What three requirements must a topic meet in order to be "right"?
2. What are some conditions a topic must meet in order to be right for *you*?
3. What are some conditions a topic must meet in order to be right for the congregation hearing it?
4. What should a person do if he finds his topic to be too broad or too narrow for the allotted time?
5. *When* should a speaker choose the topic of his next message?

Exercise

Instructor: Have the students write down one or more potential topics for a 10-minute sermon. These topics should meet the three requirements for a topic to be "right."

Note: In the later exercises, each student will be preparing and delivering a 10-minute sermon, using one of the topics he has chosen for this assignment.

7

Having a Goal

When I began to write my first book, *Will the Real Heretics Please Stand Up*, I enlisted the help of a friend who is a gifted writer. We got together at his trailer one Saturday afternoon to brainstorm the project. He opened up the discussion by asking me, "So, David, what's your take-away?"

"My what?"

"Your take-away," he repeated. "You know, the main thought you want your readers to *take away* with them after reading your book."

"Oh," I replied sheepishly. "Well, actually I don't have a 'take-away.' It's just going to be an informational book."

"Well, that will never do," he explained to me. "You must have a goal in mind when you write a book. There needs to be some conclusion you want to bring your readers to."

Well, thanks to his help, the book got written, and it had a message to it. A sermon is no different. It has to have a goal. You should know exactly *why* you chose the topic you did and *where* you want to take your hearers. Do you want to motivate them to change an aspect of their lives? Do you want to bring the unsaved to surrender their lives to Christ? Do you want to persuade your hearers to embrace a particular doctrine or viewpoint? Or do you want to motivate them to a particular plan of action?

You see, it's not enough merely to have a clear topic. You must have an objective in mind; otherwise, your sermon will seem pointless to your hearers.

In saying what I have, I don't mean to imply that there is no place for instructional sermons. In fact, most of my messages are primarily informative. But I try always to have a point to my messages and a firm goal in mind. I don't want my sermons simply to be a bundle of information. I want them to challenge my hearers to new ways of living or new ways of thinking. At a minimum, I want to lead my listeners to a new appreciation of God and His workings.

Imagine a group of young people attempting to play a game of volleyball. However, none of them knows what the object of the game is. So they simply bat the ball back and forth across the net—with no purpose in mind. After a while, the game would get very boring, wouldn't it? Without a goal, a sermon is the same way. It gets boring very quickly. The congregation can't figure out what the point of the message is. That's because there is no point. The speaker's primary objective is simply to bat information around for sixty minutes.

To prepare a sermon without a specific goal in mind is like building a house without any idea of what the final product is supposed to look like. No qualified builder would ever do that. If he did, he would have only a mishmash of studs, rafters, and drywall. Likewise, no servant of Christ should ever throw together a sermon without a specific goal of where he is headed.

Your goal should concern something you feel strongly about—something that excites you. By the time you finish preparing your sermon, you should have something that you just can't wait to tell your listeners.

Topic + Goal = Theme

So once you choose your subject matter, you need to unite it to a goal as quickly as possible. For example, let's say that your general topic is "Abraham." You could easily talk about Abraham for an hour. However, without some goal in mind, your hearers will gain little from your sermon. So think about where you want to take your listeners by the end of the sermon. There are numerous possibilities.

For example, your goal may be to motivate them to imitate Abraham's faith. Or you may want to help them to see how faith and obedience worked together in Abraham's life, as taught by both Paul and James. Through this, your ultimate goal may be to help your listeners grasp a better understanding of salvation. Or your goal may be to help your listeners see mistakes that Abraham made so they can avoid making the same mistakes in their lives.

Once you have united your topic to a specific goal, you have a *theme* for your message. Your theme may be "Understanding How Faith and Obedience Work Together in Salvation." Or perhaps it could be "Avoiding the Mistakes that Abraham Made." Or your theme may be "Imitating the Faith of Abraham."

Once you have developed a theme, you can give your message a title. In most churches, it's normal to state the title of your message somewhere in your introduction. Your theme and your title may be one and the same. Or you may wish to give your sermon a more thought-provoking title—one that relates to your theme, but is more captivating.

Having a topic, a goal, and a theme is like having the foundation laid for a building. You've made a significant start. But now it's time to begin constructing the walls and roof. Where do you start?

Discussion Questions

1. Why must a sermon have a goal?

2. When a goal is united to a topic, what does it produce?

3. Does the title of a sermon have to be the same thing as its theme?

Exercise

Instructor: Have each student select one of the topics from the previous exercise and write out a goal and theme for that topic.

8

Building Your Sermon

Virtually all builders follow a set procedure when they construct a house on a slab foundation. Normally the first thing a builder does is to prepare the site. Next, he pours a foundation (which includes basic plumbing). After pouring the foundation, he does the framing and builds the roof. After that, he and his subcontractors run the initial electrical wiring, install insulation, and hang the drywall. Finally, the builder oversees the finish work, such as painting, nailing trim, installing flooring, and completing the final plumbing and wiring.

Building a sermon is much the same way. There are basic steps that most experienced preachers use. I personally follow the six-step plan described below. These steps are flexible and can be adapted to your own preferences. But to be an effective speaker, you will want to follow some plan.

Six Steps to Building a Sermon

The six steps I follow when I'm building a sermon are

- Praying for guidance
- Researching
- Reflecting and brainstorming
- Illustrating my topic
- Organizing
- Sculpturing.

Praying for Guidance

I would never think of starting to prepare a sermon or write a book without prayer—and neither should you. The starting point for all Christian speakers needs to be prayer. There are things that God wants your listeners to hear that you might not ever think of on your own. He is interested in what you have to say, and He will help you if you only ask Him to do so. But don't just pray at the *beginning* of your preparation—pray throughout the entire course of it.

Researching

What reference tools should a speaker have? Actually, the only *essential* tool is the Bible. Throughout most of Christian history, men preached with no other source at their disposal than the Scriptures themselves. So don't imagine that you can't be an effective teacher without a large reference library. Having a Bible and *knowing* its contents are the primary things.

Nevertheless, other reference tools can be quite useful, such as Bible aids. Some of the Bible aids that speakers frequently use are an unabridged concordance, *Thompson's Chain Reference Bible*, *The Treasury of Scripture Knowledge*, and *Nave's Topical Bible*. A conservative Bible dictionary or encyclopedia also can be helpful.

Let's suppose your topic is "The Sin of Coveting." You could begin by looking up "covet" in an unabridged concordance. My concordance shows that a form of "covet" appears thirty-eight places in the Bible. That's a huge help. However, with a concordance, you have to look up each citation in your Bible. A concordance doesn't reproduce the whole verse.

In contrast, a Bible aid such as *Nave's Topical Bible* not only gives you the citation, but it also reproduces each passage. As a result, you don't have to look up each one separately in your Bible. In addition, in relation to our present illustration, *Nave's* provides a long list of examples of covetousness in the

Bible—such as David coveting Bathsheba and Eve desiring the forbidden fruit. *Thompson's Chain Reference Bible* and *The Treasury of Scripture Knowledge* likewise give you Scriptural references beyond what a mere concordance gives you.

As I mentioned, there are thirty-eight Bible passages that use a form of "covet." But you would hardly want to use all thirty-eight of those passages. That would bog down your sermon. So you want to select only the chief verses, the ones that will best help you develop your theme. For an hour-long sermon, five or six passages might be sufficient.

Reflecting and Brainstorming

At this point, you have a topic, a theme, and the pertinent Scriptures that will serve as the pillars of your message. What do you do now? Now is the time for reflection and brainstorming (i.e., serious thinking). As you reflect, write down everything that comes into your mind. At this point, don't worry about the order in which you place these thoughts. But I recommend either writing your thoughts on 4 x 6 cards or in a computer word processing program. This will enable you later to rearrange your reflections in a logical order.

When brainstorming, ask yourself lots of questions: What covetous practices do I have in my own life? What covetous practices have I observed in others? Why does God view covetousness as such a serious sin? What are some Bible examples of covetous persons? What are some of the foremost weaknesses in our congregation in this area? What questions would my listeners probably ask me if they had the opportunity? What resistance am I likely to meet from the congregation on this issue?

Hopefully, you've already been praying and reflecting on your theme for a number of days or weeks. Bring out any notes you've previously written down. As you build your sermon, you need to amplify and establish your theme. You do this through examples, illustrations, and applications of Bible teaching. Through these techniques, you make your theme stand out.

Your material should also be fresh, and it needs to be *you* speaking. Don't serve your listeners warmed-over material borrowed from someone else.

You also should show your listeners why your message is vital to *them*. The measure of a sermon is the effect it has on its hearers. Unless you show why your message is vital to your hearers, they will quickly forget your sermon. With your ultimate goal in mind, you need to move your listeners toward that goal with sound, convincing arguments. Don't depend upon the *manner* of your delivery to persuade them. Even if you have the ability to sway your hearers solely by your motivational delivery, the effect on your listeners will be short-lived if your arguments don't hold up to sober analysis and reflection.

Finally, as you write your outline, define your key terms. In our example above, you might want to give a definition of the word *covet*.

Now, quite often I run into a mental block somewhere midway through my brainstorming. Sometimes, I can't think of anything more to say about my topic or any new direction to explore. At that point, I just lay my outline down and come back to it another day. That's why I try to begin writing my outline at least a week in advance. After leaving my outline for a day or two, I usually find I can get past my former mental blocks and complete my brainstorming.

Illustrating, Organizing and Sculpturing

Sadly, many speakers end their preparation once they have assembled sufficient material through brainstorming. They provide no illustrations of their main points. And they never organize or sculpture their material. As a result, their sermons are anything but memorable. Instead, they are dull, disorganized and too long. These final steps of illustrating, organizing, and sculpturing are so important that I'm devoting two whole chapters to them.

Discussion Questions

1. Name the six steps in building a sermon.
2. Why should someone pray for guidance before preparing his sermon?
3. What is the one essential reference tool for a sermon?
4. Name some helpful Bible study aids for sermon preparation.
5. Describe a method for brainstorming—either the one described in this chapter or a method you have developed.
6. What should a person do if he reaches a mental block when he is brainstorming?

Exercises

a. **Instructor**: Using the topic and theme he has previously selected, each student should research that topic in preparation for a 10-minute sermon.

b. **Instructor**: After researching his topic, each student should brainstorm his topic and theme and write down his thoughts on 4 x 6 cards or on a computer.

9

Illustrations Make a Sermon Memorable

Jesus was the greatest teacher who ever walked on our planet. One of the things that made Him such a great teacher was His frequent use of illustrations. Everything He taught his hearers about God, prayer, holy living, and the kingdom of God, He explained through illustrations. His disciples followed His example, and their letters are likewise filled with illustrations. Today, as disciples of Jesus, we should imitate Him—not only in the way He lived, but also in the way He preached. Illustrations typically make the difference between an interesting, memorable sermon and a boring, quickly forgotten one.

Illustrations can take many forms, including examples, analogies, anecdotes, statistics, historical information, visualizations of events, interesting quotations, stories, case histories, and parables. Your sermons should abound in illustrations, just as Jesus' sermons did. The reason He used illustrations so abundantly is that they are the lifeblood of any sermon. In fact, they serve three important functions in a spoken message:

- They help your listeners to understand.

- They engage your listeners.

- They aid your hearers to remember what you said.

Illustrations Help Your Listeners Understand

The most effective way of explaining a spiritual truth to your listeners is through an illustration. Analogies from abstract concepts to common things in everyday life can help your audience grasp matters that are complex. For example, Jesus helps us to understand God better by comparing Him to a loving earthly father. He helps us understand the workings of the kingdom of God through countless illustrations: The kingdom is like a field of wheat and tares. It's like a mustard seed that grows into a large plant. It's like a treasure hidden in a field. The list goes on and on.

Illustrations keep your sermon from being superficial and vague. When you don't use examples, analogies, and case histories, your listeners just won't get the point. You must get specific! And illustrations enable you to do that. I well remember the story my mother told me about President Calvin Coolidge when I was little. The President had attended church one Sunday, and afterward a reporter asked him what the preacher had spoken about.

"Sin," was his terse answer.

"Well, what did he say about it?" the reporter queried.

"He was against it!" was the President's brief reply.

That may be all your listeners will be able to say about your sermon as well if you don't get specific with examples and other illustrations.

Illustrations can also help to *persuade* your hearers. An apt story will help win your listeners over to some point they would otherwise resist. Illustrations in the form of background information can enrich your hearers' knowledge of the Bible.

Illustrations Engage Your Listeners

Illustrations not only help your listeners understand your message, but they also help you to hold their attention. Remember, it's not natural for people to sit for an hour while someone else does all of the talking. You have to purposefully add "spice" to your message to keep everyone's attention. And please don't use the excuse that "you're not there to entertain; you're there to preach." Jesus didn't entertain people, but He *did* make His sermons graphically clear and interesting.

Imagine your favorite dish without any spices. How would it taste? Take spaghetti and meat sauce, for example. What if your wife made spaghetti and sauce for you but left out all the spices, saying that they were "unnecessary." So she simply served you spaghetti topped with plain tomato paste and browned ground beef. No salt, no pepper, no oregano, no basil, and no mushrooms! On the one hand, it would have basically the same nutrition as her regular spaghetti and meat sauce. On the other hand, you probably wouldn't enjoy it very much, would you? It certainly wouldn't be a memorable meal.

A sermon is the same way. You can have a sound, meaty message with lots of spiritual nutrition. But if you don't add some "spice" to it, your listeners will struggle to pay attention. It won't be a memorable message. Illustrations are the spice that capture your listeners' interest. I can think of numerous instances when I was listening to a tedious sermon and struggling to keep fully attentive, when suddenly the speaker said, "This reminds me of a time when..." Suddenly my ears perked up, and the speaker had my undivided attention again.

Illustrations Help Your Listeners to Remember

Experts tell us that an audience usually will forget 95% of what they hear and retain only 5%.[1] So you should be thinking to yourself, "How can I help my listeners remember what I preach?" The answer is: "Use illustrations." Illustrations not only kept Jesus' messages interesting, but they also enabled His disciples to *remember* His teachings. What people remember the best about Jesus' teachings are His illustrations and stories. Even non-Christians know what we're talking about when we mention the "prodigal son" or the "good Samaritan."

Your sermons, too, will be remembered if you use excellent illustrations. When someone tells me they remember something from a sermon I gave years ago, it's nearly always an illustration they remember. Similarly, when I think back on the thousands of sermons I've heard over the years, the primary things I remember are the illustrations that various speakers used.

How Do You Come Up with Illustrations?

"But where does a person get his illustrations?" you might ask. To answer that, let me ask you a question: "Where did Jesus get *His* illustrations?" He obtained them from everyday life, didn't He? Furthermore, Jesus drew on the common things of life for His illustrations, not the exceptional. As I mentioned earlier, Jesus was an *observer*. He noticed all the small everyday occurrences of life. He observed the behavior of children, parents, farmers, various tradesmen, and religious leaders. If your sermons are going to be rich with illustrations, you must be an observer like He was.

Again, I must emphasize the need for beginning your preparation as far in advance as possible and earnestly praying for God to help bring illustrations to your mind. Like many of you, I'm not particularly gifted at coming up with illustrations. If I started preparation on Saturday night for the next morning's sermon, I would probably have no illustrations to share. Illustrations just don't come to me easily. However, if I reflect and pray on a subject long enough, I invariably do come up with illustrations. But they usually come to me when I'm doing something else—such as mowing the lawn or lying in bed.

I often find that if I discuss a sermon topic with my wife or friends, an illustration sometimes comes to me during the conversation. Or perhaps one of *them* will think of an illustration I can use. At times, just in the course of reading something entirely unrelated, I come upon something that will make a good analogy or anecdote. Occasionally, something another speaker says in his sermon starts the gears of my mind working and an illustration pops into my mind during the middle of someone else's sermon. For that reason, I almost always bring a notebook to church with me so I can write down illustrations and ideas before I forget them.

Avoid "Processed Illustrations"

You can find a number of "illustration books" that will provide you with analogies, anecdotes, and other sermon illustrations. However, I encourage you *not* to get your illustrations from such books. The best illustrations are homemade ones. Stories from "illustration books" are like processed frozen meals that a person can buy at the grocery store. They're better than nothing, but they can't begin to compare with a home-cooked meal. After all, what do you prefer: homemade mashed potatoes or the instant kind?

When I was in my thirties, I attended a church whose pastor had a gift for teaching. His illustrations were marvelous, and he always had lots of them. All of them came from his own observations and personal experiences. However, he eventually moved, and a young preacher who had recently graduated from seminary took his place. It was obvious that this young preacher got most of his illustrations out of "illustration books." They were rarely personal. The contrast between him and the previous preacher was enormous. His illustrations were like instant mashed potatoes.

If you truly have the desire to be an effective speaker and make it a subject of earnest prayer, God will help you learn to develop illustrations. After all, virtually everyone uses anecdotes in personal conversation—without even giving it any prior thought. You only need practice and God's help to see how these anecdotes can also effectively communicate truths in your sermons.

When I was a young boy in my pre-teens, I belonged to a sect that trained its young men to be public speakers. Each

week one of the boys my age would deliver a five-minute public Bible reading at the midweek service. He would also present
a brief introduction before the reading and a short conclusion
after it. Like most of the boys my age, I always had my mother
prepare the introduction and conclusion for me. That's because
I assumed I didn't have the ability to do so.

However, at one of the services, a boy my age delivered a
really striking introduction and conclusion to his reading. I later
learned that he had prepared it himself. Suddenly, I realized that
perhaps *I* could write my own introductions and conclusions.
So I began doing so. Soon I found that I could prepare much
better ones than those prepared by a third party.

It's the same with illustrations. You *do* have the ability
(with God's help) to prepare your own. You only have to recognize and believe that you have that capability—and then put
this inherent ability into practice.

The Legitimate Use of Books

There are some legitimate uses of reference books to obtain
"spices" in the forms of examples and historical information.
For instance, as I've mentioned, *Nave's Topical Bible* lists Biblical examples of covetous people. A brother preparing a message on covetousness would no doubt find these useful. Case
histories from the Bible are not a substitute for personal examples, but they will add both meat and interest to your message.

Congregations are always interested in hearing about the
customs of people in Bible times: their manner of dress, mar-
riage observances, daily habits, and customs of trade. Bible
dictionaries and encyclopedias often can provide that information. And your hearers will be grateful that you have expended
the time and energy to acquire that information for them.

Biographies of prominent Christians and books with missionary accounts or hymn stories can provide rich information
that will fit into certain sermons. Even secular books can pro-

vide you with fertile material. Learning about animals and
plants can provide you with illustration possibilities. After all,
many of Jesus' illustrations concerned plants and animals.
Books on archaeology, geography, science, art, and music all
can provide information that you will one day be able to put to
good use in sermon illustrations.

Other Illustration Sources

Your own imagination can furnish rich illustrations for your
sermons. If you can't think of a true-life story that illustrates
your point, perhaps you can make up a story that illustrates it.
Jesus did that all of the time. The prodigal son, the good Samaritan, the unjust steward, and the persistent widow all are fictional stories that illustrate truths Jesus wanted to get across.
Your only obligation is to let your audience know that what
you're sharing is not a true story. Never pass off a parable as
though it were a real occurrence. When you're using a fictional
story, you should introduce it with a phrase such as: "Imagine
this" or "It's as if . . . ."

Helping Your Listeners to Visualize

Visualizations of Biblical scenes are a form of illustration at
everyone's disposal. Several years ago, during a sermon, a
brother read the passage from the Gospels about Jesus throwing
the vendors and money-changers out of the temple. Like most
other Christians, I've read that passage many times. In fact, I
could practically quote it from memory. But this brother added
something very special to that passage—he helped us visualize
the scene at the temple courtyard: "Imagine what it was like in
the temple courtyard," he said. "Cows were mooing and sheep
were bleating. The smell of animals and manure filled the air."

You know, I had never thought about that before. A wor-
shiper going to the temple had every right to expect to be
greeted with the sounds of fervent prayers and the smell of
incense. Instead, the sound of farm animals and the smell of a

barnyard greeted him. And he would have had to watch where he stepped!

Now, that was a small thing this speaker added to that account. But through his brief visualization, he helped me to picture a scene that I had never fully thought about before. I'll probably remember his visualization for the rest of my life.

Any one of us can do the same thing with other Bible scenes. Help your listeners experience the sights, sounds, and smells. You don't have to fabricate anything. Just use common sense and your own experiences.

For example, none of us has ever spent a year in an ark with a bunch of animals. But we've all been to a zoo or a farm before. It doesn't take much imagination to picture what it sounded and smelled like in the ark. Do you think Noah and his family were getting a bit fidgety by the end of that year? Without a doubt.

Using Visual Aids

Most humans learn more through their eyes than they do through their ears. I know that I do. As I mentioned earlier, experts say that audiences only retain about 5% of what they *hear*. But what they *see* will remain with them much longer. That's why visual aids can be helpful.

A visual aid can take a number of forms. In its simplest form, it can be merely a blackboard or marker board. One of the brothers in our congregation often begins his messages by writing a brief outline of his sermon on the marker board. This is an enormous help, as it allows the rest of us to follow the course of his sermon as he develops it.

Overhead projectors enable you to show information to your listeners that would be too time-consuming to write on a blackboard. I've often used overhead projectors to display charts, lists, and long quotations from historical sources.

Now, not every church is comfortable with a speaker using visual aids in his sermon. So make certain you know how your church feels about visual aids before using them.

Taking the Next Step

Once you've added examples, stories, and other illustrations to the sermon you're building, you're a long way toward your final goal. You now have all your material gathered. However, at this point, it's still merely an unorganized mass of information. So you have to take your sermon to the next step: organization.

_____

[1]Ronald L. Willingham, *How to Speak So People Will Listen* (Waco, Word Books, 1968), p. 58.

Discussion Questions

1. What made Jesus' messages so memorable?

2. What three functions in a sermon do illustrations serve?

3. According to experts, how much does an audience normally retain from a spoken message?

4. Name some methods and sources for developing illustrations.

5. Why should "illustration books" normally be avoided?

6. What is visualization and how can it enhance a sermon?

7. What are some commonly used visual aids?

Exercises

a. **Instructor**: Have each student develop one or more illustrations for the 10-minute sermon he has been preparing.

b. **Instructor**: Each student should orally deliver a visualization for one of the following Bible passages (or a passage of his own choosing):

(1) Gen. 43:15-34   (2) Gen. 11:1-9   (3) Ex. 12:29-34

(4) 1 Kings 18:20-40   (5) Matt. 14:22-33

10

Organizing and Sculpturing Your Material

If you want to be an effective speaker, you have to organize your material. Otherwise, your listeners won't be able to follow where you're going. Even if you have put considerable preparation into your sermon, if it isn't organized it will still sound to the congregation as if you're just rambling.

The First Step of Organization

At this point in your preparation, I'm assuming you have all of your material written out on 4 x 6 cards or on a word processing program. As the first step of organization, with your theme and goal in mind, divide your material into three parts: the material that should logically go near the beginning of the sermon, the material that should fit towards the end, and the material that would logically fall somewhere in the middle.

The Second Step

After you've done the simple organizing of step one, review your material. Then divide your material into: (1) main points and (2) minor points that support the main ones. Make sure that your material thoroughly develops the main points with Bible verses, supplemental information, applications, and illustrations. It's important that each main point further develops your theme and leads your listeners toward your ultimate goal. Rearrange your main points (with their attached minor points) into a natural, logically flowing order.

Sculpturing Your Sermon

A writer once told me, "Writing is like sculpturing. You normally start off with far more material than should be in cluded in your book. You then have to start cutting away and eliminating much of your material until you have the final product." Preparing a sermon is no different.

So it's important that you don't have too many main points. For a sixty-minute sermon, limit yourself to four or five main points. For a ten or fifteen-minute devotional, you should have no more than three. If you have more than those in your initial outline, you need to do some sculpting.

There are several reasons why you should limit your main points to these recommended numbers. One reason is that if you have too many "main" points, none of them will stand out. You will end up overwhelming your listeners with too much information. They will not remember what the main points of your message were. You'll probably also end up having to rush through your sermon to finish on time. Furthermore, when you have too many main points, you'll end up failing to develop them properly.

Having Too Much Material

If you have prepared far enough in advance and have brainstormed thoroughly, you may well end up with too much material. That's actually a good problem to have. It allows you to select the very best points out of your assembled material. So don't become so sentimentally attached to your material that you can't bear deleting any of it. An effective speaker must learn to be ruthless, carving away at his material until he has just the right amount for his allotted time.

How do you know what to eliminate and what to retain? If you can't accomplish the purpose of your message without certain material, then it needs to stay. On the other hand, if any material can be eliminated without weakening the purpose of the sermon, then that material isn't essential. If there's room within the allotted time, nonessential material can stay—so long as it adds value to your sermon and makes it more engaging. However, if it's irrelevant or would bog down your sermon, then it should go, regardless of whether there's time for it or not.

The Appetizer and Dessert

At this point, you've gathered your material, enriched it with illustrations, organized, and sculpted it. Your sermon is now nearly complete. However, it still needs an appetizer and dessert.

Discussion Questions

1. Describe the first step in *organizing* your sermon material.

2. Describe one or more other steps of organization.

3. What does it mean to "sculpture" your material?

Exercise

Instructor: Have each student organize the material he has been preparing. Also have each one sculpture his material as needed.

11

Rousing Introductions and Conclusions

The introduction and conclusion of your sermon are like the appetizer and dessert of a meal. A meal certainly can exist without them, but an appetizer and dessert go a long way to making a meal really special. It's the same with your introduction and conclusion.

Even though the introduction is the first thing you'll say in your message, it should be the *last* thing you prepare (along with the conclusion). The reason is that you can hardly prepare an introduction to a message that doesn't yet exist. So first prepare your message, organize your material, and sculpt it down to its final size. Then, after you know exactly what points you'll be covering, begin working on your introduction and conclusion.

The Introduction

The introduction needs to accomplish two purposes:

● Capturing your hearers' interest

● Letting your hearers know the subject of your message.

Don't take for granted that your listeners are automatically interested in your subject. You have to *get* them interested. And if you don't do this at the start, it's unlikely you'll be able to capture their interest later. There are a number of ways to seize the attention of your listeners:

1. Start off with an interesting story or illustration.

2. Begin with a stirring quotation or a bold statement, such as: "One man has said, 'Mammon is the largest slave-holder in the world.'"

3. Make a startling prediction, such as: "Within twenty-five years, it may be a crime in this country to speak against homosexuality."

4. Ask a question or two for your hearers to think about: "What would you do if someone broke into your house and threatened to kill your family?"

5. Inject a hypothetical situation: "Suppose the government passed a law in this country making it illegal to preach against abortion."

6. If your sermon is primarily an informational one, you can begin by telling your listeners that they will be learning things that most Christians don't even know.

7. Mention a recent news event that has caught most people's attention—if it relates to your topic.

The main thing in all these approaches is to involve your audience at the very beginning. Let them see how your message is going to benefit and bless them personally. Create anticipation.

The second thing your introduction should accomplish is to let the congregation know exactly *what* you'll be speaking about. You should state the theme or title of your message, and then provide a simple list of the major points you'll be covering. But keep all of it brief. Don't end up boring your listeners with a long, wordy introduction.

The Conclusion

What you say *last* is often the *first* thing people remember about your sermon. For that reason, having a good conclusion is extremely important. There are two things you want to accomplish in these final minutes:

(1) Provide a brief summary of what you've said, and

(2) Stir your listeners to action.

By reviewing the main points of your message, you help your listeners tie everything together in their minds. It also helps them remember your main points. But this should not be a lengthy review. The conclusion should be brief—perhaps four or five minutes long at the most.

But reviewing your main points is not the only thing you want to accomplish through your conclusion. You also want to drive home the goal to which your message has been leading. Jesus ended His Sermon on the Mount with an illustration that made it clear what He expected His hearers to do: "Many will say to Me in that day, 'Lord, Lord, have we not prophesied in Your name, cast out demons in Your name, and done many wonders in Your name?' And then I will declare to them, 'I never knew you; depart from Me, you who practice lawlessness!' Therefore, whoever hears these sayings of Mine and *does* them, I will liken him to a wise man who built his house on the rock" (Matt. 7:22-24).

Be like Jesus. At the end of your sermon, tell your listeners exactly what you want them to do. Don't hem and haw around. Get right to the point and say it with conviction. Never end your sermon by merely trailing off with some scattered, off-the-cuff "concluding remarks."

"Circling the Airport"

Imagine a pilot who has nearly reached his destination and begins his landing approach. However, just as he's about to land, he suddenly pulls up and flies back into the air. He then circles the airport a number of times. Finally, he begins to land once more. Yet, again, just as it appears he's going to land, he unexpectedly swoops back up in the sky. How do you suppose his passengers would feel?

A good friend of mine likens this scenario to a speaker who indicates that he's about to conclude his message, but then keeps going on. He repeatedly says, "in conclusion ..." —but to the dismay of his listeners, he invariably aborts his landing and pulls back up in the air. Never do that. Prepare your conclusion carefully, so you can wrap up your sermon in a few minutes in a carefully chosen manner.

Memorization

As we discuss in the next chapter, you should never attempt to memorize your entire message. You want to *converse* with your hearers, not deliver a memorized or scripted speech. However, I do recommend that you memorize your first few opening statements and the last few concluding ones. You don't want to be at a loss for words at those two crucial points in your message. Nor do you want your head buried in your notes. You need to be looking directly at your listeners. You should speak in an arousing manner when you begin your message, and you want to speak with a tone of finality when you close it.

Your Speaking Outline

Once you've prepared your introduction and conclusion, your sermon is complete. You have an organized, logically flowing message, with a striking introduction and conclusion. It might seem that you can finally stop at this point. In fact, many speakers do. And then they end up wondering why their sermons are boring and why so many people are sleeping while they preach on . . . and on!

Discussion Questions

1. *When* should a speaker prepare his introduction and conclusion?
2. What two purposes should an introduction accomplish?
3. Give some examples of ways a speaker can capture his listeners' attention in his introduction.
4. What two things should the conclusion of a sermon accomplish?
5. What is meant by "circling the airport"?
6. What portions of his sermon might a speaker want to memorize?

Exercise

Instructor: Have each student prepare a brief introduction and conclusion to the sermon he has been working on.

12

Your Speaking Notes

As I've said several times, your goal is to have a *conversation* with your listeners. You can hardly converse with them if your head is buried in a written manuscript or a detailed outline. So the final step of preparation is to write an abbreviated outline of your sermon. I will refer to this abbreviated outline as your "speaking outline."

Extemporaneous Speaking

Virtually all good speakers today speak extemporaneously. The term *extemporaneous* has several meanings. One meaning is speaking "impromptu"—with little or no preparation. That's definitely not the type of extemporaneous speaking I'm talking about. What I mean by *extemporaneous* speaking is that you are not going to be reading your message from a script, nor will you be memorizing it. In fact, when you get up to speak, you won't know the exact words you're going to say (except for your opening and closing statements). But you will know the *ideas* you want to present. You just won't know the precise phrasing you're going to use.

Does that sound scary? It shouldn't. You do it every day. When you chat with a friend, do you know in advance the exact phrasing you'll be using? Of course not. In fact, you often don't even know the *topic* you'll be discussing. The words and ideas just flow naturally. That's how conversation works. You've been doing it almost your whole life. Most people can converse extemporaneously for hours without any preparation at all.

An extemporaneous sermon is in some ways easier than an ordinary conversation because you know exactly what your topic is and where you're headed with it. You know what points you're going to develop—and even the order in which you're going to discuss them. What's more, you know ahead of time the stories or illustrations you'll be giving. The only thing you don't know are the exact words you will use.

Because you're going to be having an extemporaneous conversation with your listeners, all you need in the way of notes is an outline that reminds you of all the ideas you want to get across. You don't need a word-for-word manuscript. But how do you know what you need to include in your speaking outline and what you can safely leave out? I'll share with you the method I use.

My Method of Preparation

The initial outline that I type up as I'm preparing a sermon usually is quite detailed. It won't work well for a speaking outline because it's too wordy. It would be hard to find my place in it as I'm speaking.

So the first thing I do is to print out the initial outline from my computer. I read over this initial outline several times to make certain that all of the points and thoughts contained in it are impressed on my mind. I then read over it another time, using a yellow marker to highlight the key points of the message. I don't highlight entire phrases or sentences. Instead, I highlight only the key words.

Next, with this highlighted outline in front of me, I try to see if the main substance of my message comes to my mind without having to look beyond what I've highlighted. If I'm not able to do that, I read over my initial outline again until I know it better. Then once again, I look at nothing but the highlighted material to see if I can now recall the substance of the sermon without looking beyond what I've highlighted. If I find there are still some points I'm having trouble remembering, I then go back and highlight in yellow those other points as well.

Once I'm satisfied that I can recall my entire message just from what I've highlighted, I then type up my final speaking outline, including only the items highlighted in yellow. When it's time to speak, I want to be looking primarily at my hearers, not at my outline.

Characteristics of a Good Outline

Obviously, you don't have to follow my exact method for preparing your final outline. If you have a different way that suits you better, by all means use it. Nevertheless, your speaking outline must have the following two qualities:

- It must be readable at a glance.

- It must contain enough information to bring the points and illustrations of your sermon to mind—without tying you inordinately to your notes.

We've probably all experienced the situation of sitting in church listening to a sermon, when suddenly the speaker pauses, squints his eyes, and tries to decipher his notes. Meanwhile, those of us in the pews sit there awkwardly as the speaker tries to figure out his notes. Few things detract from a sermon as much as that.

So never write out your outline in longhand. If you don't have a typewriter or computer, then *print* it out by hand. The main thing is that your outline is highly legible at a quick glance.

To this end, I normally place all my major headings in extra large print. I also leave several lines of blank space at the end of each main section of my message. That way, each section stands out. Often, I go back over my final outline and highlight in yellow all the illustrations—just to make sure I don't somehow overlook them while speaking.

But What If I Forget Something?

Inexperienced speakers often hesitate to speak from a brief outline from fear they'll leave out something. Well, I'll let you in on a secret: I almost always leave something out when I speak. But so what? My listeners don't know what was in my original notes. So they're not aware that I forgot to say something I had planned to say. And there's no law that says everything in a speaker's outline has to be said. So don't worry about forgetting something.

Now, I have never left out a main point of my sermon or an important illustration, because those things are well marked in my outline. And if you've prepared properly, you won't forget those things either. Everything indispensable to your message must be included in your speaking outline, and the main points need to stand out in some way.

Guidance of the Spirit

Earlier in this book, I talked about the Holy Spirit guiding a speaker. One of the beautiful things about extemporaneous speaking is that you're able to include anything the Spirit may bring to your mind as you're speaking. From time to time, I've had splendid illustrations suddenly pop into my mind when I'm speaking. Since an extemporaneous speaker is not bound to a written manuscript or memorized message, he is free to use insights that flash into his mind.

Practicing

Unless you're already a seasoned speaker, I strongly encourage you to practice your messages *out loud*. Just mentally reviewing your outline is not the same.

Some books suggest that you practice your sermon in front of a mirror. If that works for you, then by all means do it. However, it may make you feel too self-conscious. If so, just practice in a room by yourself. If you have a wife, teenaged son or daughter, or friend willing to listen to you, then that is even better. For they may be able to give you helpful feedback.

When you practice your sermon out loud by yourself, I recommend that you put in front of you both your original complete outline and your final speaking outline. As you practice, look only at your speaking outline. But if you get stumped or realize you're forgetting too many things, then go back and look at your fuller notes.

If you're able, practice your message out loud in this manner until you can deliver the full message just from your speaking outline. If you keep finding that you're unable to do that, then you need to broaden your speaking outline to include those matters that you're having trouble remembering. Modify your outline and keep practicing until you can preach from your speaking outline alone.

Is This Too Much Work?

At this point, you may be thinking to yourself, "This is way too much work!" My response is: it all depends upon how much value you place on being an ambassador of Christ. If you think preaching a sermon is a trivial thing, and you just want to get it over with as soon as possible—then, yes, this is too much work.

Let's go back to the same question I asked earlier in this book: Is that the same view you take of your secular work? If you're a carpenter, mechanic, or some other tradesman, do you think it's too much work to do things properly? Do you view your work as a trifling thing, something to get out of the way as quickly as possible? If not, why do you treat the Lord's work in a different manner?

Actually, if we're talking about preparing a devotional, the amount of preparation time required is still fairly small. And if you start far in advance and spread your preparation out over a period of days, the time taken out of your daily schedule is fairly minimal.

The good news is that you will eventually reach the point at which you will no longer need to practice your messages out loud. I haven't practiced a sermon out loud in years. And I don't know of any experienced speakers who do. But I practiced all of my devotionals and sermons out loud when I was younger, and I'm glad for it.

Preparation Is the Key

In the chapters ahead, we'll be talking about *delivering* your message. But before we go there, I again want to emphasize that one of the primary attributes that distinguishes an effective message from a mediocre one is preparation. If you want to be of the most use to Christ, if you want to bless your brothers and sisters with a worthwhile message—never skimp on preparation. Even once you become an accomplished speaker, you'll still not be able to redeem a message that has been poorly prepared.

Discussion Questions

1. As used in this book, what is meant by "extemporaneous speaking"?

2. Why should a person not try to speak from a written manuscript or detailed outline?

3. Name a method for reducing one's initial detailed notes into a shorter speaking outline.

4. What two characteristics should a speaking outline have?

5. Why should a person not write out his speaking outline in longhand?

6. Describe a method for practicing a sermon out loud.

Exercise

Instructor: Have each student use his detailed notes to prepare a speaking outline for his 10-minute sermon.

13

Be Yourself

If I could give you only one rule for delivery, it would be this: *Be yourself.* We're blessed to live in an age when listeners appreciate speakers who are simply themselves. In the nineteenth century, the speakers that audiences appreciated the most were orators, such as Daniel Webster. Men were trained *not* to be themselves when they spoke in public. They were expected to take on a certain aura of grandiosity.

But things changed in the twentieth century. People came to appreciate speakers such as Will Rogers, who were simply themselves. A number of factors brought about this change. One was the invention of the microphone. Speakers no longer had to shout to be heard. They could speak in a normal, conversational voice and still be heard by everyone in the audience. Another factor was the further shrinking of class distinctions among people. Grandiloquent speakers who put on pompous airs and elevated themselves above their listeners were no longer appreciated. Listeners wanted to hear someone who was a "man of the people."

As I said, this change is a blessing. You can truly be yourself, and your listeners will appreciate you for it. They don't want you to take on a new persona when you get behind the pulpit. They want you to be who you are. Your ordinary everyday language is quite sufficient. There's no need to put on airs.

Accordingly, as you prepare your message, put yourself—your personality and method of speech—into your outline. Stamp your personal imprint on it. A sermon by you on "loving your enemies" should sound different from a sermon delivered by someone else on the same subject. The truths and basic meaning should be the same, but not the way you present it.

I think we all appreciate the variety of personalities in our churches and families. This same variety should be evident in our speakers. As one writer has observed, "When we copy others, we typically end up copying their faults, not their virtues."[1] Variety actually can add zest and life to our sermons. So express your message in your own way. Use your everyday language. Don't refer to yourself as "we," or use other such artificial speech. If you don't have a lot of education, don't try to cover it up by being artificial, stiff, and formal. Your listeners will love you for who you are.

Improving Yourself

Now, when I encourage you to be yourself, I don't mean that you can't make improvements that will enhance your ability as a speaker. For example, if you normally mumble when you speak, you'll want to work on speaking clearly—both in everyday life and when preaching. If you speak too softly, you'll want to work on speaking louder. If you normally speak with little animation in your voice, work on speaking with more enthusiasm. Remember, you're an ambassador of Christ around the clock. Poor speech habits detract from your ambassadorship.

Similarly, if you use poor grammar or mispronounce certain words, you'll want to work to correct these matters both in everyday speech and in public speaking. If you normally dress slovenly, you'll want to work on changing your dress habits. Your aim should be to eliminate any blemishes that make you less useful to Christ. But none of these changes mean being someone other than yourself. They simply mean improving what you already are.

If there are improvements you need to make in your grammar or everyday manner of speaking, pray about these changes constantly. Entreat God to enable you to overcome any grammatical or speech defects you may have.

At the same time, don't become self-conscious about various shortcomings in your speech. Work and pray to improve your everyday speech, but don't become so concerned about your speech defects that it scares you from speaking in front of a congregation. An earnest message delivered by you in a sincere manner will be far more effective than a message given by someone with impeccable grammar whose message lacks sincerity and the power of the Holy Spirit.

---

[1]William Evans, *How to Prepare Sermons* (Chicago: Moody Press, 1964), p. 16.

Discussion Questions

1. What is one of the most important rules for delivering a sermon?

2. What are some common speech defects a person should try to correct?

14

Speak Conversationally

The ultimate expression of being yourself is speaking conversationally. And the wonderful thing is that none of us have to *learn* how to speak conversationally. It's something God has built into us. It's something we naturally do. Even small children can carry on conversations.

But it never ceases to amaze me how so many speakers suddenly become stiff and artificial—and even pompous—once they begin preaching. I think many men imagine this is what they're supposed to do when they preach. They believe that the more they shout, the better their message is.

Speaking conversationally begins with proper preparation. If you've prepared a "speech" rather than a conversation, then you're hardly going to sound conversational. Likewise, if you're reading your sermon from a written manuscript, you won't be conversing with your listeners either.

Why You Should Speak Conversationally

There are several reasons why you should speak conversationally in your sermons. To begin with, it's the normal way that Jesus and His apostles spoke. Jesus used everyday speech when He was teaching. He didn't use language familiar only to the intellectual elite. And he didn't give oratorical, wordy speeches. His apostles spoke similarly. Paul told the Corinthians, "For Christ did not send me to baptize, but to preach the gospel, not with wisdom of words, lest the cross of Christ should be made of no effect" (1 Cor. 1:17).

Second, except when hearing extremely gifted orators such as George Whitefield, most people find it far easier to listen to someone speaking naturally and conversationally than they do listening to someone who speaks stiffly and artificially. Few people fall asleep during a conversation with a friend. So the more conversational you are in your delivery, the less likely it is that your hearers will get sleepy.

The fact is that—whether it's listening or reading—most people prefer simple, everyday expressions to eloquent, artificial language. This is nicely illustrated by the contrast between two conservative American magazines: the *National Review* and the *Reader's Digest*.

The *National Review* is an eloquently written journal with many multisyllabic words unfamiliar to the average person. Not surprisingly, it has only about 155,000 readers, which is not very large for a prestigious, national magazine. Since its inception more than fifty years ago, the *National Review* has never even made a profit. Donations still keep it afloat.

In contrast, the *Reader's Digest* is purposefully written at a high school reading level. It uses familiar words and relatively short sentences. It has probably never won any literary awards. Yet, it has a readership exceeding 78,000,000—the largest circulation of any magazine in the world. And it's printed in 21 different languages. In short, people prefer everyday, conversational language to polished literary diction.

In everyday life, we all know how to speak conversationally. But, ironically, most of us have to learn how to do so when speaking in public.

How to Speak Conversationally in Public

The secret to speaking conversationally in public is to focus on *ideas*, not on *words*. The words will come automatically. We don't even think about this process in everyday life because it is so automatic. We focus on ideas, and the words come. But most beginning public speakers focus on *words*, instead of ideas. That creates the problem. They end up trying to think of a certain word or phrase they intended to use. When it doesn't come to mind, they're lost.

Your speaking outline should be designed primarily to bring ideas to your mind, not words. You should never be at a loss for words, because you can quickly scan your outline and see the next idea to discuss. Words will come automatically once you remember the idea.

To be sure, there will be times when you want to say something in a very particular way. In that case, you may want to write out the exact words in your speaking outline and perhaps flag them in some way. Then when you reach that point in your sermon, you can look down and quickly find the phrasing you wanted to use. So long as you don't have very many of those specially worded phrases in your outline, they should be easy to find.

Conversation Includes the Eyes

Up to this point in our discussion of speaking conversationally, we've been mainly talking about vocabulary, voice quality and use of an outline. But speaking conversationally involves more than those things. It also includes what you do with your *eyes*!

Discussion Questions

1. What does preparation have to do with speaking *conversationally*?

2. Why should a person speak conversationally when he preaches?

3. What is the secret to speaking conversationally in a sermon?

Exercise

Instructor: Have a few of the students orally deliver their 10-minute sermons. Have them focus on speaking conversationally.

15

Eye Contact

I think we all know where our eyes should be looking when we're talking with someone. We should be looking right at the individual. Face to face, eye to eye. None of us enjoy conversing with someone who rarely looks at us. This is true whether we're having a conversation with one person or with a congregation of two hundred people.

You can never be an effective speaker without good eye contact. When you're delivering a sermon, you should be looking at your hearers at least 90% of the time. Obviously, you have to look down at your notes occasionally. And you don't have to try to hide the fact that you're looking at them. But you should never deliver a sermon with your head buried in a pile of notes—only occasionally looking up to make sure that your listeners are still there!

The Mechanics of Eye Contact

But how do you make eye contact with a hundred or more people? You do it one at a time. Select one person and talk to that person for ten or fifteen seconds, as though you were talking just to him or her and to no one else. However, don't gaze too long at one person, or else you'll embarrass him. Move on to someone else in another part of the room. But look at each selected person long enough to make mental contact.

Be sure to spread your eye contact around the room. Don't just speak to the persons on the front row, or in the back, or on one side of the room. Speak briefly to a person on the left side of the room, and then speak to someone on the right side. Speak briefly to people in the front few rows, and then to those in the back of the room and in the middle.

When I'm speaking, I find that much of my energy feeds off of my hearers. If they are excited about what I'm saying, it helps me to stay excited. Invariably, wherever I'm speaking, I find that the congregation has at least two or three persons in the congregation who are what I call "inspiration boosters." They listen attentively, and they usually have bright eyes and smiles on their faces.

I thank God for these "inspiration boosters." I'm sure you'll find such "inspiration boosters" in your church as well. Take advantage of their positive feedback by regularly making eye contact with them throughout your message.

When to Look at Your Notes

It's important not only that you look at your notes no more than 10% of your speaking time, but also that you don't look at them at the *wrong* times. For example, you should be looking at your listeners when you give your first few opening statements, as well as your closing ones. Likewise, as you're reaching a climactic point in your message, you need to be looking at your hearers—not your notes.

Another time you should be looking at your listeners is when you relate an illustration or story. On a number of occasions, I've observed speakers who included an interesting illustration or narrative in their messages, but they were looking at their notes nearly the whole time they shared it! This detracted enormously from what should have been a high point of their sermon.

Maintaining eye contact with your hearers not only benefits them—it benefits you as well. That's because it enables you to *listen* to them.

Discussion Questions

1. A speaker should be looking at his hearers what percentage of his speaking time?

2. How does a speaker make eye contact with an entire congregation?

3. When should a speaker *not* be looking at his notes?

Exercise

Instructor: A few of the other students should now orally deliver their 10-minute sermons. The emphasis this time should be on their maintaining eye contact with their listeners.

16

Listening to Your Listeners

At first glance, you might think that the title of this chapter must be some sort of misprint. Listening to your *listeners*? Yes, that's exactly what I mean. When you make eye contact with your listeners, you'll soon find that they're communicating back to you. They're constantly revealing their reaction to your words through their facial expressions and body language. What kind of things are they telling you?

For one thing, they're normally telling you that your message is either interesting or boring. They're often telling you whether they agree with you or not. They may be telling you that you've gone on long enough and it's time to stop. Or they may be saying that they would like to hear more. At times, they may be telling you that something else in the room or outside is distracting them. Finally, they'll usually let you know whether or not your message is getting through.

Responding to Negative Feedback

If you've chosen a good topic and are well prepared, most of the live feedback you'll get from your hearers will be positive. However, from time to time, you will invariably receive negative feedback as well. Instead of resenting such feedback, make grateful use of it.

For example, you may be trying to explain a theological doctrine, and you see a number of people with puzzled looks on their faces. They're telling you that they're having difficulty grasping what you're saying. You need to know this. It gives you the opportunity to explain things in a different way or expand on what you've already said.

What if you're not sure whether or not your hearers are grasping what you're saying? Just ask your listeners! Literally. That's the beautiful thing about extemporaneous speaking. It allows you to be spontaneous.

I frequently ask for feedback when I can't tell whether my audience is following me or not. I typically ask something like, "Are you with me, or am I losing you?" When I ask a question like that, I'm not necessarily expecting verbal replies, although sometimes I get them. But I always get some sort of nonverbal feedback. People either nod their heads or shake them. If they're grasping what I've been saying, then I move on. If they're not understanding me, then I try to break things down and make them more understandable.

When Your Listeners Disagree

If you choose your topic with reasonable care, you should rarely have the situation in which your audience takes issue with what you're saying. If you're still new to public speaking, you'll certainly want to stick to subjects that are "safe." On the other hand, if you're a pastor, you may feel God wants you to address issues that may step on some people's toes. If so, don't shy away from such topics.

I must be a glutton for punishment. For whatever reason, I find it hard to get motivated to speak unless I'm sharing something provocative to my listeners. I like to present historical information they're probably not familiar with, or have them look at a familiar topic from a different angle, or challenge them in some spiritual area. People who enjoy my books have come to expect this from me. But this same trait often gets me in hot water when I'm speaking in public. That's because my listeners in such situations aren't necessarily fond of my books.

So on more than one occasion I've found myself with a hostile audience. What should a person do in such a situation? To begin with, don't just pretend everything is fine. Try a different approach. Acknowledge that you realize many in the congregation are not comfortable with what you're saying. Sometimes you might want to directly ask your hearers what they're taking issue with. It may be that they have simply misunderstood what you've said. Perhaps you simply need to explain yourself better.

The reason you need to respond to negative feedback is that your goal as a speaker is to *persuade*, not to offend. If all you do is cause your listeners to raise their shields and tune you out, you've accomplished nothing. You want to open their minds so that they can see areas of sin in their lives or truths they've never known before.

Actually, the best time to address the situation of a hostile audience is when you're preparing. If you foresee a negative reaction to your message, then you need to carefully prepare what you say so you can get your listeners to look honestly at themselves. If Nathan had just boldly confronted David over his sin with Bathsheba, David probably would have rejected his reproof. But because Nathan approached it in a tactful and sensitive way, he got the desired results.

When You're Boring Your Hearers

Actually, the negative feedback that speakers receive most often from their listeners is not disagreement—it's boredom. If you're losing the congregation's attention, I can assure you that they'll let you know. Their facial expressions and body language will tell you. Instead of looking at you, they'll begin looking at the clock, gazing around the room, or peering out the window. Others will start fidgeting, doodling on paper, or slouching in their seats. All around the room, you'll see drowsy eyes and sleepy faces. Without uttering a syllable, your listeners are telling you that your message is uninteresting to them.

So what do you, the speaker, do? Well, if you're reading from a manuscript or trying to speak from a thick pile of notes, you'll probably keep pushing on, losing more and more of your listeners as you go. But what would you do in a real-life conversation with friends if you noticed they were getting bored? You would change the subject, wouldn't you?

That's what you have to do as a speaker. Well, sort of. I don't mean that you should tear up your outline and start speaking on a totally different topic. But you do need to do something to change the pace and direction of things. Hopefully you have an interesting illustration or anecdote that you were going to bring up later in your message. If it's appropriate, go ahead and give it now. This will help win back your audience.

Or, it may be a good time just to stop speaking and start asking questions. Perhaps you can ask some review questions on what you've already said. If no one can answer them, then maybe you need just to give a quick impromptu review. Or you can ask questions that perhaps will draw out your listeners' thoughts about the subject matter. If nothing else, you can ask everyone to stand and ask the song leader to lead a familiar hymn that fits your message. This will break the monotony that the congregation is feeling and wake them up.

One of the nice things about extemporaneous speaking is that it gives you *flexibility*. You can make adjustments as you go. You can shorten one part of your message if it isn't holding your listener's attention and spend more time on another part that better engages your listeners. You aren't tied to a memorized script or a written manuscript.

How to Prevent Boredom

Although you occasionally may have to tackle boredom in the middle of your sermon, the best approach is to prevent it from happening in the first place. Choosing a topic and theme that will interest both you and your hearers is the first step. The next step is preparing thoroughly so you have a lot of worthwhile material set forth in an easy-to-follow order. Finally, you

can enliven your message with plenty of illustrations, anecdotes, and examples. All these are things we've already talked
about.

But there's another step we haven't yet addressed: speaking
with enthusiasm. All the preparation in the world can't redeem
a bland delivery.

Discussion Questions

1. What are some of the things that listeners tell a speaker through their
   facial expressions and body language?

2. How can a speaker know if his listeners are understanding what he is
   saying?

3. What are some methods of handling a hostile audience?

4. How does a speaker know if he's boring his hearers?

5. What can a speaker do if his listeners are getting bored?

Exercise

Instructor: Have some of the students deliver their 10-minute sermons.
Meanwhile, assign the students in the audience specific types of nonverbal feedback to give each speaker through their facial expressions and
body language. (This feedback will not necessarily reflect their actual
response to the speakers' sermons.)

After speaking, each speaker should relate the various things his listeners
were telling him.

17

Speak with Life

Excitement is contagious. If you're excited about what you're saying, nearly everyone in the room will also be excited. In turn, as you interact with your listeners, their excitement will be reflected back to you, keeping your own enthusiasm alive. In contrast, if *you* aren't enthused about your message, neither will anyone else.

Speaking with enthusiasm begins with choosing a topic that excites you. If the topic is boring to you, how are you going to talk about it with enthusiasm? When you're excited about what you're saying, you will be energetic and animated in your delivery. Your excitement will show in your facial expressions and in your tone of voice.

Have you ever had something to tell a friend that you could hardly wait to tell? I think we've all experienced that. Well, that's exactly the way it should be with your sermon. When you're through preparing, you should be so excited about your message that you just can't wait to get to church and tell everybody. Then when it comes time to preach, you *will* be enthusiastic. Never put on a mask of enthusiasm; you want to *be* truly enthused about what you're sharing.

At the same time, you don't want to keep your level of enthusiasm at the maximum pitch throughout your entire sermon. There need to be some troughs and valleys, or else you'll tire your listeners out.

Gestures

A speaker who is full of life naturally gestures as he speaks. If you watch a room full of people conversing, you'll notice that they are normally animated, smiling, and gesturing. Gesturing is not something we have to learn. It's something we do naturally, without even thinking.

Experienced, effective speakers gesture throughout their delivery. But they don't have to *consciously* try to gesture. If you're excited about your message and absorbed in what you're saying to the congregation, you *will* gesture. As one speaker put it, "Interest and conviction make a talk, not beautiful gestures. Emotional enthusiasm and strong inner feelings produce good gestures and facial expressions. ...Get busy and strengthen your interest and conviction about your subject. Become embroiled in it. Let it become a part of you."[1]

When a speaker doesn't gesture, it's a telltale sign that either he's not excited about his message or he's self-conscious and nervous. Or, often it's both. And the key to overcoming both is in the *preparation* stage. Again, you must choose a subject that is exciting to you, one that will totally absorb you when you're preaching. Second, if you have prepared thoroughly, you're not likely to be ill at ease—unless you are new at speaking.

If you're a beginning speaker and you find yourself too ill at ease to gesture naturally, there are some steps you can take. First, you can mark different places in your outline where you want to be sure to gesture. These may be points you want to emphasize, or they may be descriptive passages in which depictive gestures will be helpful. As you practice your sermon at home, try gesturing at the places you've marked. This will get you started gesturing. But, again, once you are at ease in preaching and are absorbed in your material, you will gesture naturally—just as you do in your everyday conversations.

Confidence

As with so many other aspects of delivery, confidence is primarily a product of thorough preparation. When you walk up to the lectern, you should be brimming with confidence. Not with conceit or arrogance, but with poise. You should be thoroughly convinced that your listeners will be blessed by what you have to share. And you should have the self-assurance that you know your material thoroughly.

In fact, in most situations, you should have the confidence that you are in the position of a teacher. If you've properly prepared, it means that you will be speaking on a topic for which you're eminently qualified to speak. You may be a farmer with little advanced education. Nevertheless, if you're living a godly, Spirit-led life, you have all of the qualifications you need to talk about virtually any aspect of Christian living. If you're not living a godly life, then you probably shouldn't be speaking in the first place.

Conviction

Conviction is closely associated with enthusiasm and confidence. To speak with conviction means to speak from the heart about something you really believe in. If you don't feel passion about your subject, why should anyone bother to listen to you? So when you speak, don't pussyfoot around—hemming and hawing, apologizing, hedging, and approaching everything timidly.

It's not hard to guess how the term *pussyfoot* came into the English language. During the winter, we let our cat and two dogs inside our basement at night to sleep. First thing in the morning, I open the outside door of the basement to let them out. The two dogs go dashing out without any hesitation. However the cat just sits and looks at the door for awhile. Then she slo-o-o-wly creeps toward the door. However, she then stops and looks around. Next, she takes a few more steps toward the door, but stops short of it once again. I can't figure out if she wants to go out or stay in. Finally, after an agonizing wait, she makes it halfway through the doorway, but then stops again. I usually have to scoot her the rest of the way out.

Some speakers are like that. They say something, but then they backtrack. Next they go forward, but then they start hemming and hawing. At the end of their message, they haven't convinced anyone of anything.

Don't you be like that. If you're going to preach against something, then *preach* against it. Make sure you're on solid ground and be convinced in your own heart. Then preach like you really mean it. Don't mince words. Your listeners should know that you believe every word you're saying.

Some Points of Caution

A disciple of Christ can speak with confidence and conviction and yet be humble. Listeners appreciate a confident speaker. But they detest an overbearing, pompous one. "Do you see a man wise in his own eyes? There is more hope for a fool than for him" (Prov. 26:12). When carried to an extreme, confidence becomes arrogance. Be confident. But don't elevate yourself above your listeners.

I want to give you another word of caution. Before you boldly address the spiritual failings of your listeners or problems in your church, make sure you have the *standing* to say what you do. A pastor or elder in the church normally has the standing to speak to the congregation in such a manner. But a young man in his early twenties usually does not. If you're a young man, you should discuss such matters privately with your pastor or elders. They're the shepherds of the congregation. You're not.

Be Sure of Your Facts

When I talk about speaking with conviction, I'm referring to believing in your message and showing it by the manner in which you speak. Conviction is a good thing; dogmatism is not. We have the right and need to speak with conviction where the Scriptures plainly speak. But we don't have the right to paint things with a broad black and white brush—if the Scriptures have painted them gray. There is nothing wrong—in fact, there is a moral obligation—to acknowledge that a difficult verse can be understood in more than one way. But don't build your message around verses that are ambiguous.

Furthermore, if you're going to be adding background information to your message and interjecting other extra-biblical "facts," make certain they are *facts* and not just hearsay. There are few things I find as offensive as some speaker spouting out a lot of "facts" when in reality he doesn't know what he's talking about. Either make *certain* of your facts, or don't use them.

Never Speak in a Boring Voice

If you're speaking with enthusiasm, confidence, and conviction, it's unlikely that you'll have any problems with speaking in a boring voice. However, because so many speakers fall into the trap of speaking in a monotone, I want to talk more in detail about that.

Discussion Questions

1. What is the secret to a speaker's being able to gesture naturally?
2. Confidence is primarily a product of what?
3. What does it mean to speak with conviction?

Exercise

Instructor: Have a few other students now deliver their sermons. Have them focus on speaking with enthusiasm, confidence, and conviction.

18

Speak with an Interesting and Clear Voice

Throughout this book, I've emphasized the theme that effective public speaking is a form of organized conversation. In daily conversation, we seem naturally to know how to make our voice pleasant and interesting. We rarely speak in a monotone when talking to friends. But somehow when we're in front of a congregation we forget to do what comes naturally. That's why every speaker needs to consciously speak with modulation.

Modulation

My dictionary defines *modulation* as "a change in stress, pitch, loudness, or tone of the voice." Most people use modulation in their everyday conversations without even thinking about it. When you're wrapped up in a conversation, sometimes you raise your voice. Other times, you speak softer. You speed up at times and slow down at others. You emphasize certain words or sentences. And you vary your tone, depending on the point you're trying to get across.

But many public speakers talk in a monotone and never vary their pace. That's because they're ill at ease and perhaps overly tied to their notes. The good news is that you can overcome this problem through practice. Before you prepare your final speaking outline, go over your material and highlight the places in your message you want to emphasize through your volume and tone of voice. Also, highlight places where you should speed up and places where you should slow down. Then practice out loud before your wife or someone else, focusing on those places you have highlighted in your outline.

One of the best ways to practice modulation is to read the Bible out loud at every opportunity. My family and I try to read a portion of the Bible every night in our home, taking turns reading out loud. Very likely you and your family do the same. Use this occasion to practice modulation in your reading. Emphasize certain parts of the Scripture by speaking louder or more deliberately. Practice reading some portions faster and other passages more slowly. Observe all the punctuation in the text.

Likewise, when you're asked to read a Scripture out loud in church, use that occasion to purposefully practice modulation. Use every opportunity to master this necessary speaking skill.

Volume, Tempo, and Pausing

In everyday conversation, you usually don't have to think much about your volume. Normally, you're close to your listeners and they can easily hear you. Or, if they're having trouble hearing you, they'll immediately tell you.

However, in public speaking, you have to give conscious thought to be sure you're speaking loud enough so that everyone in the room can hear you. So at the very beginning of your message, make it a point to look at the people on the back rows to see if they're straining to hear. Once you know you're being comfortably heard, you probably don't have to think about it any further.

The advent of the microphone has made it much easier for public speakers to talk conversationally and still be heard by everyone. But ministers preached for centuries without microphones, so microphones certainly are not essential. If you're speaking in a building without a microphone, you'll have to speak considerably louder than you would in an ordinary conversation. Once again, look at the back rows to see if the people there seem to be hearing you all right. If you're not sure, there's nothing wrong with simply asking, "Can everyone hear me?"

Even with a microphone, you normally want to speak a bit louder when delivering a sermon than you would in ordinary speech—particularly if you're a soft-spoken person. You'll also want to speak a little slower than you do in everyday speech. You're imparting more serious information, and you don't want your listeners straining to keep up with you.

It also will help your listeners if occasionally you purposefully pause. This will allow what you've said to sink in. Because you will need to be looking at your notes from time to time anyway, use those occasions to insert pauses in your message—for your benefit and for the benefit of your listeners.

But that shouldn't be the only time you pause. You should occasionally use dramatic pauses to emphasize a point in your sermon or to draw particular attention to a word or phrase in a Scripture passage. I've heard experienced speakers pause midway through a sentence, building suspense in their hearers' minds until they finally finish the sentence. This technique can be overdone, but if used occasionally it will grab your listeners' attention.

Enunciation

To enunciate means to speak your words distinctly and clearly. In other words, don't mumble or run your words together. Speak a little bit slower and more distinctly than you do in everyday speech. After all, if your listeners can't understand you, they'll soon lose interest.

We've all been in conversations in which we had to stop someone and ask him to repeat what he said because he slurred his words and we couldn't decipher what he said. But no one is going to interrupt your sermon to ask you to repeat yourself. So you need to be extra careful to enunciate your words.

Almost to the Finish Line

It will take time and the delivery of quite a few sermons or devotionals to master everything we've talked about up to this point. However, all these things are within the reach of virtually every Christian. That's because most of the things we've discussed are things we do naturally in everyday conversation. If you're having difficulty mastering some of these things, fall on your face and earnestly seek God's help in these matters. Remember, you're *His* representative. He wants you to speak effectively.

Once you're adept at using the things we've discussed in your public speaking, you're almost guaranteed of having a lively, interesting and informative message. I say *almost*, because there are five things that still can trip you up before you reach the finish line.

Discussion Questions

1. What is modulation?

2. What are some ways that a speaker can practice modulation?

3. Does a microphone eliminate the need to speak louder and slower?

4. Why should a speaker occasionally pause?

5. Define enunciation.

Exercise

Instructor: Have each student select a chapter from the Bible and be prepared to read it aloud to the class. Have them practice reading with modulation and clear enunciation. Each reader should include a few pauses for punctuation and emphasis.

19

Five Things That Can Spoil an Otherwise Good Sermon

Imagine a bridegroom at his wedding who is meticulously dressed and groomed. However, unbeknown to himself, he has a large splotch of red spaghetti sauce on the front of his dress coat. Now, do you suppose people will be thinking about the 99% of him that is nicely groomed—or about the 1% of him that has the spaghetti sauce? They'll be thinking about the spaghetti sauce, won't they?

Similarly, you can follow all of the directives I've given in this book, but still have your sermon ruined by certain distracting things that are like splotches of spaghetti sauce on your sermon. These things may seem relatively minor to you, but they aren't so minor to your hearers. These five things are

- Mispronouncing words
- Poor posture and distracting movements
- Inappropriate dress and slovenly appearance
- Using "word whiskers"
- Going over your allotted time.

Mispronouncing Words

It should go without saying that you need to be sure about the pronunciation of all words you'll be using in your sermon. One mispronounced word—particularly if it's an obvious one and is central to your message—can distract your listeners from what you're saying.

The worst case of mispronunciation I've ever heard occurred when I was a teenager living in Texas. The speaker was giving a sermon on the subject of discipline. The problem was that he mispronounced the very topic of his message. For sixty minutes he went on and on about the importance of dih-SIPP-lin. I doubt any of us heard much of what he had to say. It was just too hard to get past the big red splotch of dih-SIPP-lin every few minutes.

You are more likely to mispronounce words when you're reading a passage of Scripture. Even if you don't rehearse any other part of your sermon out loud, I urge you to read all of your Scripture passages aloud beforehand. This will alert you to any words you're not certain how to pronounce.

The words in Scripture that are most apt to trip you up are names of people and places. A Bible reference work often will give you the correct pronunciation. If you can't find the pronunciation anywhere, call up someone in your church who is more likely to know the pronunciation or who has the resources to find it.

But other words in the Scriptures can cause blunders, too. I remember once hearing a speaker reading from 2 Peter 3:3 in the course of his sermon. In the King James Version, this passage reads: "Knowing this first, that there shall come in the last days scoffers, walking after their own lusts." But in the translation the speaker was using, this verse reads: "For you know this first, that in the last days there will come ridiculers with their ridicule, proceeding according to their own desires."

Now, I have no idea how the speaker made it as far in life as he had without knowing how to pronounce the word *ridicule*. But unfortunately he had. He read, "In the last days there will come rih-DIK-yool-ers with their rih-DIK-yool." I don't remember anything more of his sermon after that point. That's because the effect of mispronouncing a commonplace word like *ridicule* is like a fire alarm suddenly going off in a schoolroom.

Anything else the teacher might try to say about the lesson is totally lost because everyone's mind is on the fire alarm. Likewise, much of what the speaker says after such a pronunciation blunder is probably going to be lost to his listeners.

What's more, mispronunciations cause you to lose your credibility. Your listeners begin to wonder whether you really know what you're talking about. After all, how much confidence would you have in an auto mechanic who couldn't pronounce the parts of an engine? What if he told you, after examining your engine, "It looks like I'll need to clean out your car-BURR-eh-ter"? Would you trust him to do the job?

Poor Posture and Distracting Movements

Your posture should normally be a bit more formal in public speaking than it would if you were standing around talking with some of your friends. For example, among friends, it might be perfectly proper to sit down on the edge of a piece of furniture. But when delivering a sermon, it will look totally out of place if you sit down on the corner of the speaker's table.

You should stand up straight, though in a relaxed manner. It will detract from your message if you stand artificially stiff, like a soldier guarding Buckingham Palace. On the other hand, you shouldn't continually lean on the lectern as though you don't have the energy to stand up.

Some churches don't want their speakers to move about when they speak. They want you to stand still behind the podium or lectern. If that's the decorum expected by the church where you're speaking, then you should honor that.

In other churches, no one minds if you move about a bit, as would be normal in most conversations. After all, it's a natural thing to move a little bit when you're standing for an hour. So in many churches, it's perfectly proper for you to occasionally stand to one side of the lectern and speak from there—and then later move to another position. However, you don't want to pace continually back and forth, like a zoo animal in its cage. Most of your listeners will find that distracting. Likewise, you don't want to sway to and fro like a pendulum.

If you're not sure how your church feels about your moving about, it would be good to discuss this with your pastor *before* you speak.

Inappropriate Dress and Slovenly Appearance

What should you wear when you're speaking? The answer is: whatever is considered appropriate at the church where you're speaking. Some churches will expect you to wear a dress coat; others will expect you to wear only an appropriate dress shirt. If you're not certain what is expected, talk with the pastor ahead of time. You never want the kind of clothes you're wearing to detract from your message.

An unkempt appearance also will detract from your sermon. So make certain that your hair is combed and your clothes are ironed. If your shirt has a button-down collar, be sure to button your collar. Otherwise, someone will be thinking about your unbuttoned collar or your wrinkled shirt rather than about your message.

Using "Word Whiskers"

"Word whiskers" are the extra little words or phrases that many speakers add to the beginning or end of their sentences. Some examples are "uh," "and uh," "and now," "okay," and "you see." The last three phrases I just mentioned can be properly used occasionally throughout your message. But if every other sentence begins or ends with these phrases, they've become word whiskers. Some speakers end most of their sentences with a conjunction—such as "and" or "but"—even though they don't have anything to follow the conjunction. The conjunction just trails off into empty space: "and....."

When you're speaking extemporaneously, it's easy to fall into the habit of adding word whiskers to your sentences as you're thinking about what you want to say next. This has been a lifelong problem for me. All my life, I've had to work on eliminating "uhs" from my sermons. In fact, I still haven't completely conquered the problem. However, I've been able to bring it under control. Here are the things that helped me to get control of word whiskers. These steps may be of help to you as well:

1. *Find out if you're using word whiskers.* Usually a speaker is totally unaware of the word whiskers he uses. I know I was. I became aware of the problem only when my wife told me that I use "uh" a lot in my sermons. Even then, I didn't totally realize how bad the problem was until I heard a recording of one of my sermons. When I did, I was in absolute disbelief. It didn't seem possible that I could fit so many "uhs" in such a short span of time.

Therefore, I recommend that you listen to a recording of one of your devotionals or sermons sometime. Don't be discouraged if you find numerous word whiskers. It's a familiar problem that most of us have had to work through. Knowing you have the problem is the first step toward conquering it.

2. *Have a desire to overcome the habit.* Once I became painfully aware of my word whisker problem, I knew I had to overcome it if I was going to be very useful to God as a teacher. If you don't have an earnest desire to eliminate your word whiskers, you'll never overcome them. If you're struggling to overcome word whiskers, pray fervently about the matter.

3. *Slow down and don't be afraid of silence.* When I analyzed my own situation, I realized that the main reason I was saying "and uh" so much was that I was deathly afraid of a silent gap in my speaking. To be sure, I regularly paused for emphasis and to give natural breaks in my messages. But I was

afraid of having an unexpected pause while I was waiting to think of what I wanted to say next.

However, I finally realized that I had to accept these bits of silence. It was part of extemporaneous speaking. I don't doubt that there are speakers so fluent that they never have to grasp for thoughts as they speak. But I'm not one of them, and you may not be either. So realize that it's okay to pause now and then to collect your thoughts together. Momentary silences here and there are not a distraction. Word whiskers are.

4. *In your notes, remind yourself of the word whiskers you want to avoid.* For several years, at the top of every page of my speaking outlines, I wrote the word "uh" in huge letters. This alerted me not to use this word whisker. Eventually, I no longer had to write "uh" on my outlines. Through God's help, I had finally brought the habit under control.

To be sure, I still use the word occasionally in my speaking. In fact, there is nothing wrong with using it once in a while. Remember, your goal is to speak conversationally, and we all use a word whisker once in awhile in our daily speech. It becomes distracting to your listeners only if you use it much more than you would in ordinary conversation.

5. *Keep monitoring yourself.* Once you have your word whiskers under control, you'll want to make certain they never come back. So keep asking for feedback from your wife or friends to make sure you haven't started using your favorite word whiskers again. Or occasionally listen again to a recording of one of your messages.

Going Over Your Allotted Time

Imagine that you're flying from New York to Dallas. Everything has gone perfectly: The plane left the airport on time. The pilot skillfully minimizes discomfort by flying under or over spots of air turbulence. The flight attendants are friendly, and the beverages are refreshing. The pilot is so helpful that he points out various places and geographical features as you fly over them. In fact, he's so absorbed in pointing out places of interest that he ends up taking longer than he was supposed to, and the plane arrives at the Dallas airport late. As a result, you miss your connecting flight. What would otherwise have been a perfect flight has been marred.

Going over your allotted time is much the same way. Your message may be nearly perfect in every other respect, but if you preach longer than you are supposed to, you can quickly lose the good will of your listeners. For that reason, I've decided to devote a whole chapter to the issue of timing.

Discussion Questions

1. Name the five things that can spoil an otherwise good sermon.

2. In what ways does mispronunciation detract from a sermon?

3. What should be the posture and dress of someone preaching?

4. What are "word whiskers"? Name some of the common ones.

5. What steps can a speaker take to control word whiskers?

Exercises

a. **Instructor**: Have several students read aloud various chapters from the Bible. While each student is reading, have the other students listen carefully for any mispronunciations.

b. **Instructor**: Have a few students deliver their 10-minute sermons, with the focus on their pronunciation, posture, dress, and use of word whiskers.

20

Landing Your Plane on Time

I have one uneasy feeling about this book being published: the fear that the next time I get up to speak, everyone in our congregation will be holding up copies of this book for me to see—opened to this chapter. Yes, I myself often fail to land my own plane on time.

The irony is that I know exactly what steps to take to avoid going overtime. The only problem is that I don't always put these steps into practice. There are four steps that every speaker (including David Bercot) should follow to stay within his designated time:

1. Know how long your message is supposed to be and choose a topic that can reasonably fit into that time frame.

2. After assembling your material, whittle it down to a size that will easily fit within the allotted time.

3. Keep track of the time as you speak.

4. Speak from a flexible outline.

In the earlier chapters of this book, I discussed the first two steps: choosing the right topic and whittling your sermon down to size. So now I want to focus on the last two steps.

Monitoring Your Time

To monitor your time while you're speaking, you have to plan in advance. After you've prepared your final speaking outline, clearly identify in the margins where you *should be* when one-fourth, one-half, and three-fourths of your time have elapsed.

Then, as you speak, when you reach each of those time markers, glance at the clock to see if you're on target. For instance, let's say that you're delivering an hour-long sermon and you began speaking at 11:00 a.m. When you reach the one-quarter mark on your outline, the time should be 11:15. If you look at the clock and find that it's 11:20, you have a problem.

Now, the human tendency is to be optimistic that somehow the rest of the message will take less time than it's supposed to and that all will work out in the end. Don't fool yourself. It almost never turns out that way. If your first quarter-section took twenty minutes instead of fifteen, the same will probably be true of your second section—and of your third and fourth sections. You either will go extremely overtime, or you're going to end up having to rush through the last portion of your message, leaving out much of what needed to be said.

So what's the remedy? The remedy is to have a flexible outline that allows you to make deletions as you go.

Speaking from a Flexible Outline

It's not enough merely to mark on your outline where you should be at the end of each quarter. You also need to review your outline in advance and decide which portions can be deleted if you're overtime at any of the designated bench-marks. Then you should flag with an asterisk or a colored highlighter the parts of your message that you can eliminate if needed. Don't fall in love with your own outline. Accept up front the fact that you may have to eliminate parts of it as you speak. *Do it in advance.* Don't wait until you're in the middle of your sermon and you're in a time jam.

Of course, preparing a flexible outline will be of no help unless you learn to be *ruthless* in cutting out these expendable parts of your message, as you speak. Don't wait until the end of the sermon to make cuts. Make them after each benchmark, as needed. To be able to do this, be sure you have flagged expendable points in each quarter-section of your outline.

In short, don't spoil an otherwise memorable message by failing to get your passengers to their airport on time. Remember, when you exceed your allotted time, you end up not accomplishing your objective. Your listeners will begin to fidget in their seats, and many of them will quit paying attention. You won't have their full attention when you finally reach the climax of your sermon.

Brief Sermons That Are Too Long

Often a sermon or devotional can be too long even when you haven't gone over the allotted time. As one person told me, "I've heard a lot of twenty-minute sermons in my life, but most of them took sixty minutes." If you've said all the worthwhile things you have to say, then briefly conclude and *sit down.* Don't stand on the platform and ramble just to use up more time. If you've used up less time than you were expected to use, then resolve that in the future you will be better prepared.

The Final Barrier

In the next chapter, I'm going to discuss speaker's fright. I saved this issue until the last because it's the final barrier that lies between most of us and the ability to be effective speakers.

Discussion Questions

1. Name four steps speakers can take to stay within their allotted time.

2. How can a brief sermon still be too long?

Exercise

Instructor: Have the remaining students deliver their 10-minute sermons. They should focus on the various aspects of delivery they have been learning, including staying within the allotted time.

21

How to Handle Speaker's Fright

I think we all would enjoy public speaking if there were no such thing as speaker's fright. Yet, there it is—always hanging around, always trying to intimidate us. But don't let it.

I'm fairly certain that you suffer from speaker's fright. I say that because almost all of us have it. Think about some of the poised, confident speakers you admire and to whom you enjoy listening. I can assure you that virtually every one of them has speaker's fright. I don't mean that they *used to* have it when they were just beginners. I mean they still have it every time they get up to speak.

So I'm not going to teach you how to *overcome* speaker's fright. I myself don't know how to overcome it. But I want to teach you how to *handle* it so it won't be an obstacle to your being an effective speaker.

Just like you, I suffer from speaker's fright. I've been preaching sermons for more than forty years, and I've had speaker's fright for all of those years. When I was young, my hands literally trembled when I got up to speak. I tried to avoid gesturing during the first few minutes of my messages for fear that my hearers would see my trembling hands.

My hands no longer tremble when I speak, but speaker's fright continues to dog me like a shadow. On most Sunday mornings, my alarm clock normally wakes me up. But not on the Sundays when I'm scheduled to speak. On those Sundays,

I'm so wired up, I always wake up before the alarm. My stomach churns, and I have little appetite for breakfast.

My typical Sunday morning routine is to drink a Coke or a cup of coffee so that I'll be alert throughout the service. But I never do that on the Sundays I'm scheduled to speak. So much adrenaline is pumping through my veins that there's no danger of my becoming sleepy!

These symptoms stay with me all through Sunday school. And they're still there when I walk up to the podium and get ready to speak. And, then suddenly, after I say my opening words, they all vanish. The churning in my stomach stops, and I soon feel quite at ease. Before long, I'm totally immersed in my message, and the rest of my delivery becomes an enjoyable experience.

To be more accurate, I shouldn't say that my speaker's fright vanishes. I should say that it *changes*. It changes from fright into pure energy. It helps give my message excitement and emotion.

At the beginning of this book, I mentioned that I really enjoy preaching, and I always feel excited when our pastor asks me to speak. You may be wondering how that's possible after I've just described to you the speaker's fright that engulfs me on the mornings when I'm scheduled to speak. Perhaps an analogy will help me to explain.

When I was ten, I used to swim at a pool that had a twenty-foot-high diving board. I don't go to public swimming pools anymore, but my experience with that high diving board makes a good analogy to preaching. Jumping off of that high diving board was the main thing I liked about swimming. And, yet, it was a scary experience.

I would eagerly climb up the narrow metal ladder of the diving board, following the boys ahead of me. However, once I got near the top of the ladder, suddenly it wasn't so fun. The ground seemed so-o-o far down, and I realized that I could easily be killed or seriously injured if I fell. The fact that the rungs were wet and slippery didn't help matters any. Yet, I couldn't go back down because now other boys stood beneath me on the ladder.

Finally, it would be my turn to reach the top and walk out on the narrow diving board. As I would stand there shivering, I would invariably think, "Why am I doing this? This isn't fun; it's *scary.*" I would resolve right then and there that if I lived through the experience, I would never get up on the high diving board again. Then, because I had no other choice, I would run to the end of the board and fling myself into empty space.

Suddenly, all fear turned to fun. For a few seconds I felt like I was flying. It was an exhilarating feeling. Finally, with a whoosh, I would hit the cool water and speed downward through it like a torpedo. In a few seconds, I would be back up to the surface, smiling with glee.

What about my decision never to jump off the high diving board again? I had now completely forgotten about it. I would eagerly run to get back on the high dive. And then I would go through the same fear cycle again—only to lose it once I was in the air.

For me, public speaking is just like that. It's always scary right before I get up to speak, but it's an enjoyable experience once I plunge into it. And after I finish speaking, I've totally forgotten my earlier speaker's fright. I'm ready to preach again at the next opportunity.

Steps to Controlling Speaker's Fright

There are six steps that will help you handle speaker's fright. To be sure, you won't bring it under control the first time you speak. However, if you follow these steps, you should be able to bring speaker's fright under control:

1. Pray about it.

2. Focus on your listeners rather than on yourself.

3. Prepare thoroughly.

4. Speak extemporaneously.

5. Use speaker's fright to your advantage.

6. Know how to handle memory lapses and bloopers.

Step One: Pray About It

If you're having trouble controlling speaker's fright, make it a constant subject of prayer. God wants to use you as His ambassador. If speaker's fright is holding you back, He cares about it. Talk to God about it and ask for His power to help you keep speaker's fright under control.

Step Two: Focus on Your Listeners

To control speaker's fright, you need to understand *what* you're afraid of. What is it that scares you? Your brothers and sisters in Christ? But they're on your side. They *want* you to succeed. You're certainly not going to be afraid of them once the service is over.

So what *does* frighten you? Being the center of attention? Maybe. But even more so, what you probably fear the most is failure. You instinctively want the approval of others. But you're afraid that you will get up there and forget what to say. Or that you'll make some embarrassing blooper. Or maybe you'll just be plain boring, and people won't like your message.

What do all of these fears reveal? They reveal that you're too concerned about *self.* The remedy? Quit thinking about yourself and focus on your listeners instead.

Remember, you're not there to make a speech and to win plaudits from the audience. You're not trying to build a reputation for yourself. You're there to impart some useful knowledge, admonition, or insights to your brothers and sisters. Your focus needs to be upon *them* and upon Christ, whom you're representing.

You're not competing with other speakers to see who can give the best sermon. We're all on the same team, working to promote Christ and His kingdom and to edify God's people. I can assure you that the more you're focused on your listeners, the less speaker's fright you will have.

Step Three: Prepare Thoroughly

One of the main things you can do to minimize speaker's fright is to thoroughly prepare. When you're well prepared, you can stand behind the lectern with confidence, knowing that what you have to say will bless your hearers. You have mastered your material, and you know that you'll be sharing insights, illustrations, and exhortations that your listeners will appreciate. Thorough preparation and the confidence that derives from it squelches fear.

Step Four: Speak Extemporaneously

At first glance, it might seem that you'd have less speaker's fright if you had a complete written manuscript in front of you, instead of speaking extemporaneously. To be sure, if you read from a prepared manuscript, there's little chance of having a memory lapse. On the other hand, you've pretty well guaranteed that you're going to be delivering a boring message. Your listeners probably won't be paying close attention.

In contrast, when you speak extemporaneously, you'll soon be engrossed in an engaging conversation with people you love. And you'll find the experience enjoyable. Yes, you may leave out something and you might even get tongue-tied. But these should be of no more concern than they would in any other conversation. My experience has been that once I'm absorbed in my conversation with my listeners, my speaker's fright soon disappears.

Step Five: Use Speaker's Fright

It may sound strange, but you actually can use speaker's fright to your advantage. Why? Because speaker's fright and the adrenalin rush it produces represent pure energy. As one speaker has said, "Let the excess physical energy *help* you speak rather than hinder you in speaking. . . .Derive from it an urge and a zest that keep you from being listless and apathetic."[1]

Step Six: Handling Memory Lapses and Bloopers

A number of brothers have told me that the thing they fear the most is suddenly having their mind go blank in the middle of their message. They fear they won't remember what to say and that the whole thing will turn into a disaster. I can't promise you that you'll never have memory losses or commit bloopers when speaking. But I can assure you that they don't have to ruin your message. You just have to know the secret of how to handle them.

----

[1]Batsell Barrett Baxter, *Speaking for the Master* (Grand Rapids: Baker Book House, 1954) p. 12.

Discussion Questions

1. Do most experienced speakers still suffer from speaker's fright?

2. Name six steps that will help to bring speaker's fright under control.

3. What is one of the *causes* of speaker's fright?

4. How does extemporaneous speaking help to control speaker's fright?

22

The Secret of Handling Bloopers and Memory Lapses

Have you ever been in the middle of a conversation with someone when you suddenly forgot what you were about to say? Probably so. Have you ever become tongue-tied when conversing with a friend? Possibly so. Have you ever said something backwards or committed some other blunder in a conversation? Undoubtedly you have.

Now, did any of those miscues ruin your day or destroy your conversation? Of course not. Are you afraid of conversing with your friends out of fear that you might have a memory lapse or commit some verbal blunder? Certainly not. You realize that such things are no big deal. In fact, verbal slips often inject a light moment into a conversation.

It's no different when you're speaking in public. Bloopers and memory lapses are no big deal. As soon as you realize they're no big deal, you can conquer the fear they've held over you.

Don't Try to Hide Your Blunders

Many years ago, a young visiting speaker came to preach in our local congregation. The young man was preaching from a large set of notes rather than from a simple outline. Suddenly, in the middle of his sermon, he came to an abrupt stop. He began madly leafing through his notes on the lectern, but he didn't find what he was looking for. Then, without saying anything, he walked off the platform and went to his seat, where he had a briefcase. He opened his briefcase and began hurriedly rummaging through it, with papers flying. Apparently he still didn't find whatever it was he was looking for.

So, without saying a word, the young speaker rushed out the front door of the church. We all began whispering to one another, wondering if he had decided just to go home or something. A minute later, the young man walked through the front door triumphantly holding a fistful of papers. He then went up to the lectern and continued his sermon as though nothing had happened. Unfortunately, by that point, he had lost our good will and attention.

To this day, I still wonder *what* that man was thinking? Did he somehow imagine that nobody noticed that he wasn't still standing at the lectern? Did he think that none of us were aware he had just walked out the door?

What should the minister have done? He should have *enjoyed* the moment. He could have given the congregation a big smile and said something like, "You're not going to believe this, but my biggest nightmare has just come true. Somehow I'm missing a big chunk of my notes. I'll tell you what—why don't we all stand and have the song leader lead us in a hymn. While you're singing, I'm going to check my briefcase and then my car. If I walk out the door, I'm just going to my car. Don't worry—I'm not going to drive off and leave you."

If he had done that, we all would have commiserated with his predicament. We would have immediately bonded with him. He would have had our good will. In the end, his sermon would have ended up far more memorable than if the blunder had never happened.

Sadly, however, many speakers do just what that young man did. When they mess up, they somehow think they have to pretend that nothing happened. This causes everyone embarrassment and ends up distracting the congregation. All the speaker had to do was to admit his blunder to the congregation and move forward.

Enjoy Your Blunders!

If you make a small insignificant verbal miscue, just go on. More than likely nobody even noticed it. If it's too obvious to ignore, then *enjoy* it. People love to hear a speaker laugh at himself. I often get tongue-tied when I'm talking. When it happens, I usually say something like, "Oops! That didn't come out quite right. Let me try it again." And then I repeat it slower so that I say it correctly the second time.

The secret to handling bloopers and memory lapses is simply to enjoy the moment and refuse to be embarrassed. I find that bloopers actually break the ice and help me build a bond with my listeners. It's part of having a good conversation together. As strange as it may seem, bloopers actually can add spice to a message.

The Dreaded Nightmare: Memory Lapses

Probably the single biggest horror that inexperienced speakers fear is forgetting what they're going to say. But there's no need to have this dread.

I don't mean that you won't ever have a memory lapse. Rather, I mean you don't have to view it as some great horror. As I said in the previous chapter, we all have memory lapses from time to time in ordinary conversation, and it's never a big deal. It doesn't have to be a colossal thing in public speaking either. It's a big deal only if you're delivering a memorized speech. If you're rattling off something you memorized, and your mind suddenly goes blank, you're lost.

But when you know your material well, and you're having an extemporaneous conversation with your listeners, what's there to dread? As I've mentioned, virtually every time I speak, there are things that I had intended to say that I accidentally left out. So what? That's the way it is with conversations.

Remember, nobody in the room but you knows exactly what you were planning to say. If you leave something out, nobody is going to know—or care. If you reach a certain place in your outline and you can't remember exactly what you were going to say on that point, just move on to the next point.

I've seen very accomplished speakers take a five or ten-second pause in the middle of their message and study their outline to get the next several points in mind. We in the congregation didn't mind waiting. What you *don't* want to do is to stand there saying, "ah, uh, um ..." If you need some time to review your notes, calmly take the time to do it. Nobody will walk out of the building.

Safety Nets

If you have a particular problem with memory lapses or if your dread of a memory lapse really is holding you back, simply build some "safety nets" into your outline. Perhaps there's a Scripture passage that's pertinent to your topic, but that you weren't planning to read. Have it written somewhere in the margin of your outline in bold letters. If your mind suddenly goes blank, ask someone in the congregation to read that passage while everyone else follows along in their Bibles. While that is happening, you can catch your breath and review your outline. If the missing point still doesn't come to mind, just move on to another point.

Or you can select an appropriate hymn as a "safety net." Again, write the title and page number of the hymn in bold print in your outline. You might tell the song leader ahead of time that you may have the congregation sing that hymn during your sermon. Then if your mind suddenly goes blank, ask everyone to stand and sing together that hymn. While the congregation is singing, you can be reviewing your outline and gathering your thoughts.

Mishaps, Microphone Problems and Crying Babies

Mishaps

Whatever mishap occurs, never pretend that nothing has happened. Deal with it immediately. For example, if you're writing on a chalk board and you drop a piece of chalk, simply pick it up. I once saw a speaker leave the chalk on the floor because he didn't want to draw attention to his miscue. The problem is that during the rest of the sermon all of us were wondering whether he was going to accidentally step on the chalk or not. So the speaker didn't have our undivided attention during the remainder of his message.

Microphone Problems

What do you do if the microphone suddenly goes dead or begins giving a loud electronic hum or something? Again, don't pretend that nothing is happening. My experience has been that usually several brothers start running around checking the mike, the wires, and the amplifier. If you keep talking, probably no one will be paying much attention because they're distracted.

So if you experience microphone problems, just wait a few seconds to see if the problem is quickly fixed. If not, you might want to have the congregation sing a hymn. Or, you could move away from the microphone and conduct a short question-and-answer review until the problem is solved.

I still remember a microphone mishap at a large convention I attended many years ago. As the speaker began a statement, suddenly the microphone transformed his sentence into a long drawn out sequence of stuttering syllables: "Then—Mo-ses—gath—ered—all—the—con—gre—ga—tion—of—Is-rael." Many speakers would have been totally thrown off by that unexpected electronic mishap, but this minister simply smiled broadly at all of us and said, "Whew! That was hard." Everybody in the auditorium laughed.

In a few seconds the mike was back to normal, and the minister was able to finish his message. He had turned this unexpected problem into an enjoyable experience, and he built rapport with all of us through it.

Crying Babies and Other Disturbances

You can expect that during a message there will be at least some minor disturbances—such as crying babies. If it's just one baby, you probably can talk over the crying. However, if the disturbance is unusually loud, or if there are many babies all crying at once, you might want to take a brief pause to give the parents time to leave the room.

The general rule is this: If a disturbance is going to keep the audience from listening to you, then pause until the disturbance is over. This applies to situations other than just crying babies. For instance, if a fire truck roars by, you probably should pause until it has passed. On the other hand, if the disturbance isn't likely to keep the audience from following you, then ignore it. If one person walks in late, just keep talking. If thirty people walk in all at once, then wait.

What's Left?

Although this completes my discussion of preparing and delivering sermons, it doesn't complete the book. That's because in the final section of this book, I'm going to share some insights with you on

● Reading Scriptures in public

● Excelling in specific types of preaching—such as devotionals, expository teaching, and prophetic preaching

● Pet peeves of listeners

● How congregations can grow effective speakers.

Discussion Questions

1. When a speaker makes a blunder, should he try to hide it?

2. What is the secret to handling bloopers?

3. How can a speaker build "safety nets" into his outline?

4. What should a speaker do if the microphone suddenly goes dead?

5. What is the general rule for pausing in response to a disturbance?

23

Reading Scriptures with Zest

Scripture reading is the backbone of most sermons. That's because the Bible is the final authority for everything you say. Therefore, it's of utmost importance that when you read from the Bible, it *enhances* your sermon rather than detracts from it.

You may wonder how Bible reading can ever detract from your message. Actually, there are a number of ways it can. Among them are

1. Having the wrong citation

2. Not introducing the Bible passage properly

3. Mispronouncing words

4. Reading in a deadpan voice

5. Not showing the application of the Scripture, and

6. Reading too many Scriptures.

Having the Wrong Citation

Several years ago, I was listening to a sermon, and the speaker asked us to turn with him to 1 Corinthians 4:5. After allowing us time to turn to that verse in our Bibles, the brother began to read: "Therefore judge nothing before the time, until the Lord ..."

The speaker then paused and said, "No, that's not the verse." We all waited quietly as he started scanning nearby passages to find the verse he wanted to read. He then began to noisily flip through pages in his Bible. Eventually, someone in the congregation volunteered that maybe he meant 2 Corinthians.

"Oh, thank you," the speaker replied, and we all turned with him to 2 Corinthians 4:5. He then began again, "For we do not preach ourselves ..." After another pause, he acknowledged that this wasn't the verse either. After some more delay, he finally found the right verse—which turned out to be in Romans rather than 1 Corinthians.

By that time, the speaker had destroyed much of the credibility and good will he might have had with his audience. It was obvious that he had skimped on his preparation. He might as well have come up to the podium wearing a big sign saying, "I waited until the last minute to prepare this sermon."

You've probably witnessed similar situations. Few things destroy the flow of a sermon more than a speaker giving his listeners the wrong Scripture citation. And few things make a speaker look more inexperienced and ill-prepared. But that should never happen—because it's so easy to avoid.

You can prevent this from ever happening by doing the following: After you have finished your final speaking outline, go and look up every single Bible passage you have listed in the outline and make certain the citation is correct. That should take no more than five or ten minutes to do.

Not Introducing the Bible Passage Properly

Properly introducing a Scripture is a rather easy undertaking, but many of us have never been taught *how* to do it. There are just five simple steps:

1. Build anticipation for the passage. Before giving the citation for the Scripture you're about to read, let your listeners know why you're reading it. However, don't tell them in advance what the verse will say. Instead, build anticipation. For example, you might say, "What should be our response to evil people? Let's see what Jesus said about it in Matthew 5:39." If your listeners would be left up in the air because you failed to read the text after introducing it, then you can be sure you've aroused their interest.

2. Invite your listeners to follow along in their Bibles. This might seem obvious, but if you don't ask your listeners to follow along with you, they won't know whether you *want* them to turn to the passage in their Bibles or not. Also, if you don't encourage the congregation to open their Bibles and read along, many simply will not bother to do so.

3.   Announce book—chapter—verse. When you give the Scripture citation to your listeners, tell them the book, then the chapter, and finally the verse—in that order. That order should seem obvious, but I've heard many speakers do just the reverse. They say the verse, then the chapter, and finally the book. But we in the congregation can't start looking up the passage until we know which book the speaker is going to read from. Invariably, when the speaker uses the reverse order, he starts reading before the rest of us have found the passage.

4.   State the citation twice. There will always be some of your hearers who won't catch the citation when you first give it, or they may forget some part of it. So always state the citation twice.

5.   Give your listeners sufficient time to find the passage. You may have placed a marker in your Bible, enabling *you* to find the passage quickly. But you need to allow sufficient time for your listeners to find the passage as well. Watch the congregation carefully, and when most of them have found the passage, then begin reading.

Mispronouncing Words

Since I've already discussed mispronunciation, I'm not going to discuss the problem again in detail. But as I said before, it's often when reading Scripture passages that speakers mispronounce words. So be sure to practice reading *out loud* the verses you will use in your sermon.

If there are names or other words that you're not sure how to pronounce, then find the correct pronunciation. Once you've found the correct pronunciation, you might want to write it out phonetically on a Post-It note. I often do that myself. I then attach the note to the Bible page where the verse is located. That way, when it comes time to read that passage, I have the correct pronunciation right in front of me.

Reading in a Deadpan Voice

The Bible is a living book that is as relevant today as it was when it was originally penned. So when you read from the Scriptures during your sermon, read with life and *expression* in your voice. You should emphasize the words on which you want to focus. How do you do that? There are three common methods: (1) Reading those words louder than the rest of the passage, (2) changing your voice inflection, or (3) pausing right before and after the words you want to stress.

Never read the Scriptures in a deadpan or sing-song voice, as though you were reading from a detailed medical textbook. Likewise, never rush through the passage as though it's only a side point in your message. Scripture passages should always be the *focus* of your preaching, not merely an aside. So read them with life and zest.

As you practice reading your selected Scriptures, work on emphasizing certain words and passages that you want to stress. Keep practicing until you can read them with enthusiasm, animation, and the proper emphasis.

Not Showing the Application of the Passage

It's not enough merely to read a Bible passage well. You must also make it clear to your listeners *why* you read the passage. The application of the Scripture passage to your theme might seem obvious to *you*, but it may not be so obvious to your listeners. You must plainly point out the connection to your argument.

For example, suppose you are preaching on the topic of nonresistance and you read the passage from 2 Corinthians 10:4, "For the weapons of our warfare are not carnal but mighty in God for pulling down strongholds." Even though the connection to your topic may seem obvious, you need to clearly drive it home. You might ask, "Now, what kind of weapons did Paul say that Christians use—fleshly weapons or spiritual ones?"

Reading Too Many Scriptures

Is it possible to get too much of a good thing? Yes it is! I love German chocolate cake. If someone offers me a slice for dessert, I find it difficult to pass up. But what if someone offered me ten pieces—or fifteen pieces? No thanks. A person *can* get too much of a good thing.

It *is* possible to read too many Bible passages during your sermon. The Scriptures are the key part of your message. But, like a delicious dessert, they can be overdone. I typically incorporate five or six Bible passages in my topical sermons. If your listeners are having to constantly flip through their Bibles as you read passage after passage, you probably have too many verses.

Just heaping together a bunch of Scriptures is the lazy man's way of preparing a sermon. Anybody can do that. As I've described in this book, you should *start* with your Scripture passages and build from there. But you have to *build*. If all you give your listeners is the foundation and studs, but no walls and ceiling—you haven't preached a sermon.

Ill-prepared speakers don't expound the verses they read. They just read them, make a quick comment, and then go on to another verse. Never do that. Take the time to thoroughly expound the passages you read and then build on them. Limit the quantity of Scriptures so that you can fully develop the ones you actually use. Make certain that your listeners understand their significance and their application.

I realize that in some situations it's necessary to read a lot of verses to establish your point. This is particularly true if you're trying to establish a biblical truth that goes against the tide of what is taught in mainstream churches. There are several ways to use a large number of Scriptures in such situations without tiring out your listeners by forcing them to flip continually through their Bibles:

1. You can print out all of the verses on a transparency and display them using an overhead projector. That way the congregation can read with you all of the passages without having to turn back and forth through their Bibles.

2. You can assign several persons to read the passages out loud while the rest of the congregation listens.

3. You can have the congregation look up only a few of the key verses as you read them. The rest of the verses you can print out in your outline and ask the congregation simply to listen as you read them out loud.

Additional Issues When Reading

Reading the Psalms

The Psalms are a collection of hymns. In fact, they constituted the hymn book of the Jews—and of the early Christian church as well.

Today, our hymn books have notations to the singers or musicians, and these notations are not part of the text of the hymns. For example, in most hymnbooks you will notice that some of the hymns have the word *crescendo* written above some of the words. This tells the singers to steadily increase their volume up to a climax.

Now if you were reading the words of a favorite hymn to the congregation, you wouldn't read aloud the word *crescendo*, would you? That's simply a musical notation—not part of the vocalized text.

Similarly, many of the Psalms contain the musical notation *selah*. Like *crescendo*, this is merely a musical notation; it's not part of the vocalized text. It was apparently either telling the singers to sing louder at that point or for the musicians to clang cymbals or blow trumpets.

Regardless of the precise meaning of this obscure musical notation, it wasn't intended to be part of the vocalized text. Therefore, it's not the normal practice to read *selah* aloud when you come to it in one of the Psalms—anymore than you would say *crescendo* when reading a hymn.

On an extremely minor point, the accepted practice for introducing one of the Psalms is to say, "Let's turn to Psalm 32"—not "Let's turn to Psalms 32." It's similar to the way you would introduce a hymn. The song leader doesn't say, "Now let's turn to "hymns 32." He says, "Now let's turn to hymn 32."

Explaining Obscure Terms

The Bible contains references to various weights and measures, coins, distances, and other terms that have no English equivalent. Usually those words are left untranslated in our Bibles. For the modern reader to know their meaning, he normally has to look them up in a Bible dictionary or encyclopedia.

The problem is that people don't come to church with a Bible dictionary or encyclopedia under their arms. So when you read a passage from Scripture that contains some obscure terms, it's your responsibility as a teacher to explain those words to your listeners. Otherwise, some of the meaning of the Scriptures will be lost to them.

For instance, let's suppose that you were discussing manna in your sermon and you read Exodus 16:16: "This is the thing which the Lord has commanded: 'Let every man gather it, according to each one's need, one omer for each person.'" Now how much would your listeners get out of that passage? Not very much—unless they knew what an omer was.

So it's important for you to do your homework so you can tell your listeners the modern equivalent of an omer. According to my Bible encyclopedia, an omer was equivalent to about 1/10 of a bushel. So when you read Exodus 16:16, you need to explain that to your listeners. Even better would be to bring a container the approximate size of an omer and show it to your listeners. Now suddenly the passage from Exodus springs to life. Your hearers can picture exactly how much manna an Israelite was eating each day.

Reading from the King James Version

Several years ago, I heard a minister preaching from Proverbs against "froward" persons. He was eloquent, enthusiastic and very convicting. I saw how God detested froward persons, and I knew I certainly didn't want to be one. I was so motivated by the time the speaker finished that I wanted to go out and confront the first froward person I could find and rebuke him! The only problem was that I had no idea what a froward person was. The speaker never explained.

The King James Version was translated into the English of 1611. The King James Bible eventually became the predominant Bible in English-speaking countries. However, the English language has changed considerably over the past 400 years. As a result, many of the words used in the King James Bible are either unfamiliar to present-day Christians or have changed their meaning.

Therefore, when reading from the King James Bible, it's important that you look up any archaic or obscure words ahead of time so that you can explain their meaning to your listeners. There are a number of recent editions of the King James Bible that have been rendered into contemporary English. When you prepare your message, you might want to compare any verses you will be reading to see how these contemporary editions of the King James Bible have translated those verses. This will alert you to words whose meanings have changed over the centuries.

One example would be *conversation*. In 1611, *conversation* meant "manner of living." Today it refers to speaking. If you're reading a passage in the King James that has the word *conversation* in it, you need to explain to your listeners what that word meant in 1611. Otherwise, they'll end up misunderstanding the passage.

The Next Step

Reading the Bible aloud is probably the first step in getting acquainted with public speaking. The next step is preaching short messages, often called "devotionals." So now I want to give you some hints on preparing and delivering devotionals that will edify your hearers in a special way.

Discussion Questions

1. Name six ways that Scripture reading can detract from your message.

2. What can a speaker do to prevent giving a wrong Scripture citation?

3. What are the five steps for introducing a Scripture properly?

4. What three methods can be used to emphasize specific words in a Bible passage?

5. Is it possible to have too many Scriptures in your sermon? Why or why not?

6. If you need to use a relatively large number of Scriptures in your message, what are some ways to handle the situation?

7. When reading the Psalms, should you read aloud the word *selah*?

8. What sort of terms should be explained when reading Scriptures in your sermon?

9. When reading from the King James Bible, what is it important to do?

Exercises

a. **Instructor**: Have each student prepare a proper introduction to one or more of the following passages:

(1) Matt. 7:21-27   (2) John 13:34,35   (3) 1 Cor. 6:1-8

(4) Gal. 5:19-23   (5) Lev. 25:35-38   (6) Mic. 6:8

b. **Instructor**: Have various students read aloud the following passages, focusing on reading with expression. They should emphasize various words in these passages through volume, voice inflection, and pausing.

(1) Matt. 18:1-9   (2) Matt. 23:13-36   (3) Luke 15:11-32

(4) Acts 16:16-40   (5) Gen. 44:1-34   (6) Ps. 47:1-9

c. **Instructor**: The students should be prepared to read aloud any of the following passages of Scripture. After reading, each student should explain to the class any terms that may be unfamiliar to the class.

(1) Gen. 24:22   (2) Acts 1:12   (3) Luke 16:6

(4) Gen. 6:13-16   (5) Ezek. 45:14   (6) 1 Kings 6:37

d. **Instructor**: Each student should be prepared to read aloud any of the following passages from the King James Version and to explain any obscure terms.

(1) 1 Cor. 10:25   (2) Prov. 3:32   (3) Ex. 16:15

(4) Col. 3:5   (5) Num. 24:14   (6) 1 Sam. 21:13

24

Make Your Devotionals Special

It's a practice in many churches to begin their services with a short, five-to-fifteen minute message known as a devotional. This devotional should serve the same role for a church service as an appetizer serves for a meal.

When I eat out, my favorite type of meal is Mexican food. In Tyler, Texas, where I used to live, we had a superb Mexican restaurant called Mercado Mexicano. After you were seated there, the servers immediately brought you baskets of hot corn tostado chips, fresh from the kitchen. They also brought bowls of their delectable homemade hot sauce or salsa. The chips and salsa were so good, they whetted your appetite for the main course that was to follow. You knew you were in for a real treat!

A good devotional should do the same. It should immediately capture your listeners' interest and sharpen their appetite for the rest of the service. After hearing the devotional, the congregation should have the sense that they're really going to be blessed that morning. They should be looking forward to what's going to follow. Sadly, though, I've heard devotionals that are more like a basket of stale chips with flavorless salsa. They *dampen* everyone's appetite instead of whetting it. This gets the whole service off to a bad start.

What a Devotional Is *Not*

The purpose of the devotional is not simply to pass time until the main part of the service begins. But that seems to be what some speakers think it is. They put little time into their devotionals, usually preparing it at the last minute. Following what may have become a tradition in their church, they select a Psalm to discuss. They read the entire Psalm to the congregation, and then they go back through it verse by verse, making brief comments as they go. There's really no topic, theme or organization to their lackluster message. It's just a brief running commentary on a Psalm. That's not a true devotional.

What a Devotional *Is*

In essence, a devotional is a mini-sermon. One of its purposes is to help the congregation put aside any distractions and to focus their hearts and minds on God. If you're delivering a devotional, your job is to get the congregation focused and alert for the rest of the service. You also want to whet their appetite for what will follow. So you want to deliver a lot of punch in a short period.

There's no reason why the devotional can't be one of the highlights of the service. Typically brothers who deliver devotionals don't speak on a regular basis. That means they have more time to put into their preparation than do the main speakers in their church. Furthermore, because they're speaking for only a brief period, they have the luxury of selecting only the very best material. So their devotionals should be really special.

How to Make Your Devotionals Special

To make your devotional special, choose a topic that will immediately grab your listeners' attention and prepare them for the spiritual meal to follow later in the service. One of the best ways to do that is through a story or striking illustration. Normally a speaker prepares the framework of his sermon first and then finds illustrations to add to his framework. But with a short devotional, you actually can choose a motivating story or vivid illustration first—and then build your message around it. Of course, your story needs to have a clear purpose and spiritual message.

Earlier in this book, I talked about collecting a file of illustrations and stories. Even if the only speaking you do is giving brief devotionals, you should be thinking of illustrations every week and filing them away. Then when you're assigned to preach a devotional, you will have an abundant supply of illustrations to choose from. Pick an illustration or story that will fit nicely into a Scriptural theme and will engage your listeners. Then follow all of the steps set forth in this book for preparing and delivering a worthwhile sermon.

Building a Devotional Around a Scripture

If you would rather begin by selecting a Scripture passage, that's perfectly fine as well. But select a brief passage. Ten or fifteen minutes is not long enough to do justice to an entire Psalm or chapter of Scripture. One or two verses is more appropriate.

What's more, you should select a passage with immediate practical application. You could choose a passage of Scripture on some positive aspect of the Christian life: forgiveness, joy, thankfulness, compassion, modesty, contentment, hospitality, generosity, nonresistance, prayer, or witnessing. Or you could choose a passage that deals with a common sin or weakness— such as gossip, impatience, discouragement, envy, worldliness, or pride.

Actually, the Psalms are not the best source for a good devotional. Psalms is a book rich with meditations, reflections, and Messianic prophecies. It's a consoling book to those who are downhearted and grieving. Many of the Psalms make excellent passages to preach from at a funeral. My normal practice is to read one of the Psalms every night before going to sleep. But when you're preaching a devotional, you're not wanting to calm your listeners down to prepare them for a quiet sleep. You want to wake everyone up!

So rather than preaching from the Psalms, I recommend that you select a short passage from the Gospels or Epistles. The Epistle of James, in particular, is rich in practical teaching. The main thing is to choose a passage that allows you to preach an invigorating and interesting message. By the end of your devotional, your listeners should be awake and eagerly anticipating what is to follow.

Discussion Questions

1. Why do many devotional messages fall flat?

2. What is one way of making a devotional special?

3. Are the Psalms the ideal Bible book to use for a devotional?

Exercises

a. **Instructor**: Have some of the students prepare a 5-minute devotional built around an illustration they have thought of.

b. **Instructor**: The remaining students should prepare a 5-minute devotional built around one of the following passages:

(1) Matt. 13:45,46   (2) Jas. 1:26   (3) Jas. 1:27

(4) Jas. 5:12   (5) John 15:14   (6) Luke 9:62

25

Preparing
an Expository Sermon

Throughout most of this book, I have focused on *topical* sermons. A topical sermon is one for which a speaker first selects a topic, then builds on it using various Scriptures and illustrations. Topical sermons are the most common kind, and they are usually the easiest for beginning speakers.

But there is another type of sermon—the *expository* sermon. In contrast to topical sermons, in expository preaching, the speaker typically goes through an entire book of the Bible in sequential order over a series of many Sundays. For example, he may decide to preach on the Gospel of John. He will start with John 1:1 and preach on several verses each week in numerical order. He will continue going through John until he finishes the last verse of the final chapter of that Gospel. This could take him many months—or even years.

How to Prepare

Most of the rules for preparing and delivering a topical sermon apply to expository sermons as well. As I've mentioned previously, when preaching a topical sermon, you must select a topic that you understand and that excites you. Actually, it's no different with expository preaching.

One of the first rules of expository preaching is to prayerfully select a book of the Bible with which you are quite comfortable and in which you find a lot of material for exposition. If the message of a given Bible book isn't clear to you—and if you aren't excited about its message—then select a different book. Expository preachers don't normally start with Genesis and work their way through to Revelation. Generally, they select books that hold the most interest for them and offer a timely message for their hearers.

The Six-Step System

When in my thirties, I was privileged to sit for many years under an extremely gifted expository teacher. He made every passage of Scripture so clear and easy to understand that people began flocking to his church just to hear his teaching. Although he took his messages entirely from the passages of Scripture before him, he was always able to see a clear theme that bound each verse together. And he made his themes stand out.

What was his secret? For every sermon, he followed six simple steps:

1. *Take only one paragraph*. Regardless of which Bible book you've chosen, take only one paragraph for your sermon each week. So, for instance, instead of going through the Book of Galatians chapter by chapter, go through it paragraph by paragraph.

Now, it's important for you to understand that none of the Bible books were originally written in paragraph format (or with chapters and verses). All the subdivisions in the Bible books are man-made. So you're not bound to follow the paragraph divisions as printed in your particular Bible edition. If you see fit to make the paragraph divisions differently, then you're free to do that. The key is to group together only those verses that relate to the same theme.

2. *Break the paragraph down into natural divisions*. A Bible paragraph normally is rich in thought, and you shouldn't try to teach it to your hearers in one big bite. You have to break it down into many little bites. You might want to use each verse as a separate bite, but that won't always be the best way to divide up the paragraph.

I say that because the verse divisions in our New Testament were made in 1551 by a French book printer named Robert Stephanus. He created our verse divisions while he was traveling from Paris to Lyons, France. Consequently, there is nothing sacred about these verse divisions. So look for natural breaks in thought, ignoring the verse divisions.

Let's take, for example, the passage in 1 Corinthians 1:18-20, which my Bible prints as one paragraph:

"For the message of the cross is foolishness to those who are perishing, but to us who are being saved it is the power of God. For it is written: 'I will destroy the wisdom of the wise, and bring to nothing the understanding of the prudent.' Where is the wise? Where is the scribe? Where is the disputer of this age? Has not God made foolish the wisdom of this world?"

Now, what would be the natural divisions in this passage? There's no one right answer, but here is how I would break them down:

A. For the message of the cross is foolishness to those who are perishing.

B. But to us who are being saved it is the power of God.

C. For it is written: 'I will destroy the wisdom of the wise, and bring to nothing the understanding of the prudent.'

D. Where is the wise? Where is the scribe? Where is the disputer of this age?

E. Has not God made foolish the wisdom of this world?

3. *Write these divisions down separately on a piece of paper.* I will refer to these divisions as propositions. You might want to write each proposition on a separate 4 x 6 card, or you might want to list them separately on a single sheet as I have done above. The important thing is that you separate each of these propositions.

4. *Analyze what relationship each proposition has with the ones before it.* Start with proposition B and think about what it has to do with proposition A. Does it add further support to proposition A? Or is it in *contrast* to it? Or is it perhaps a list of subpoints? Or is it an example or illustration of proposition A?

In our passage from 1 Corinthians, proposition B is in contrast to proposition A, isn't it? "The message of the cross is foolishness to those who are perishing" (proposition A), "*but* to us who are being saved it is the power of God" (proposition B). What about propositions C, D, E? They all support the first two propositions by adding the testimony of the Old Testament, together with the observations of Paul's own readers. But each proposition further develops Paul's argument.

5. *Identify the main theme of this paragraph.* Now that you've analyzed your paragraph and broken it down into different propositions, you need to decide what is the overall message or point of the paragraph. In our example, Paul states his theme quite clearly: The message of Christ is foolish to unbelievers, but it is the power of God to those who believe.

Now, the theme often doesn't stand out this clearly in other paragraphs of Scripture. However, as you carefully analyze the writer's propositions, you will *always* be able to find a theme that ties them together. My pastor friend who uses this method has preached thousands of expository sermons over a period of more than thirty years, and he has yet to find a paragraph in Scripture without a definite theme. The inspired Bible writers didn't throw out haphazard, unrelated thoughts. They wrote with purpose and organization.

If you find a paragraph that seems to have two unrelated themes, then perhaps what you really have is two paragraphs. Remember, *you* decide where the paragraph should begin and end. And what determines a paragraph is the existence of a single, unified theme.

Once you identify the theme, make certain that you emphasize that theme as you go from proposition to proposition. However, it's not enough only to expound and emphasize this theme. You also have to show how it has a practical application to your listeners.

6. *Use examples, stories, and analogies to illustrate each proposition*. The final step is to find various illustrations to clarify and drive home each proposition. So, in our example, you will start with proposition A ("The message of the cross is foolishness to those who are perishing"). After explaining the proposition, you'll want to give analogies and examples to illustrate it. It shouldn't be too difficult to think of examples of people who look at the message of Christianity as foolishness. In fact, the whole world looks at it that way. You can probably give many examples and analogies.

Next you will move to proposition B. Again, you'll discuss it briefly and then give illustrations to clarify and establish Paul's point. From there, you'll move on to each of the remaining propositions, one by one, with illustrations for each of them, to the extent possible.

Variations

Please understand that this six-step method is *not* the only way to prepare an expository sermon. If you have another method that works well for you, then by all means use it. But I can personally testify that the six-step method is extremely effective.

One variation to the six-step approach I've outlined is to go through a Bible book one *chapter* at a time, instead of one paragraph at a time. For a long book like Genesis, this may be the more practical approach. Nevertheless, good expository speakers who use the chapter approach, still find a single theme that fits the entire chapter and they emphasize that theme throughout their sermon.

What Expository Preaching Is *Not*

I've described what good expository preaching is. Now let me tell you what it's *not*.

- It's not going through a Bible passage and simply rephrasing what the Bible writer has already said.

- It's not merely giving a running commentary on a passage, without any unifying theme.

- It's not parroting what some printed Bible commentary says.

The most common fault of inexperienced expository preachers is failing to provide a unifying theme to their messages. As a result, their "expository" sermons become an amalgamation of unrelated thoughts and insights. If you asked their hearers later that day what the sermon was about, probably no one could tell you.

The Problem with Commentaries

Some expository preachers think they must go to a commentary to expound on a Scriptural passage. The problem with this approach is that the Bible was written for the common man—not for educated theologians. You don't need a doctorate in theology or a seminary degree to understand the Bible. God has never needed human learning to spread the message of the cross. Advanced learning usually works as a hindrance, not as a help to grasping the gospel.

After all, do you think that the early Christian teachers of the first and second centuries pulled out commentaries to understand the Scriptures? I can assure you they did not! In fact, there weren't even any commentaries in existence at that time. With the guidance of the Spirit, they simply read the Scriptures and applied them literally and seriously.

And there is no reason why you can't do the same. If you are an ordinary individual, then you're the very type of person to whom the Spirit was addressing the Scriptures. Jesus told us that the gospel was hidden from the humanly "wise and prudent" (Matt. 11:25). So we don't have to go to the "wise and prudent" to understand His message. For that reason, I almost never use commentaries myself.

Let the Bible and the Holy Spirit speak to your mind and heart, and then share that with your listeners. Don't give them the warmed-over leftovers from someone else's reflections. If you don't feel comfortable or qualified to read and expound the Scriptures with the guidance of the Holy Spirit alone, then I recommend that you stick to topical preaching.

Having said that, I know that some excellent expository preachers do use commentaries judiciously. If you're going to use them, let me make this recommendation: first analyze the passage by yourself. Pray about what you read and form your own conclusions about the meaning of the passage. Only after you have done that should you go and see what some of the commentators have to say about the passage. Test and weigh their comments. Never just uncritically accept their commentary and then repeat it in your sermon.

A Variety of Gifts

I firmly believe that virtually every Christian man can learn to give effective topical sermons. But experience has shown me that not everyone is capable of giving worthwhile expository sermons. Those who have the gift and who work to develop it can bring marvelous blessings to their hearers. Many of my favorite speakers are men who preach expositorily. But not everyone has the gift. The same thing is true of prophetic preaching.

Discussion Questions

1. What is an expository sermon?

2. Describe the six-step system of preparing an expository sermon.

3. What are some things that expository preaching is *not*?

4. What is the danger with commentaries?

Exercise

Instructor: Using the six-step system described in this chapter, each student should prepare an expository outline for one of the following passages:

(1) 1 Cor. 11:2-16   (2) Gal. 3:19-25   (3) Phil. 3:17-4:1

(4) 1 Tim. 6:6-10

26

Preaching with Power: Prophetic Preaching

Throughout this book, I have emphasized the conversational nature of public speaking. However, there is an important exception to that rule: prophetic preaching. Of course, all preaching should be prophetic preaching—in the sense that all of us should preach through the guidance and power of the Holy Spirit.

But when I use the term "prophetic preaching" here, I'm referring to the *style* of preaching used by John the Baptist and many of the Old Testament prophets. John wasn't always conversational. Sometimes, he was quite pointed and forceful. Notice what he preached to the Pharisees and Sadducees:

"Brood of vipers! Who warned you to flee from the wrath to come? Therefore bear fruits worthy of repentance, and do not think to say to yourselves, 'We have Abraham as our father.' For I say to you that God is able to raise up children to Abraham from these stones. And even now the ax is laid to the root of the trees. Therefore every tree which does not bear good fruit is cut down and thrown into the fire" (Matt. 3:7-10).

When I think of prophetic preaching in post-Biblical times, I particularly think about George Whitefield and Charles Finney. In more recent times, perhaps the two best-known prophetic preachers have been A. W. Tozer and Leonard Ravenhill. I was privileged to sit under Leonard Ravenhill's preaching for several years. And I can attest to its remarkable power.

Prophetic preachers speak with a sense of dramatic urgency. Typically, their goal is to convict their hearers of sin and for the need of repentance. They don't want to make their listeners comfortable; they want to make them *uncomfortable.* They often seek to bring their listeners to a life-changing decision right then and there.

I think there can be no question but that God has used prophetic preachers in powerful ways. Lives are changed through their preaching. The work of a prophetic speaker is a high and wonderful calling. Although not every Christian man has the calling and gifts to excel in prophetic preaching, God can wonderfully use those who do.

And even for those of us who aren't called to this type of preaching as our normal ministry, there are times when the subject matter calls for prophetic preaching rather than conversational delivery.

What Prophetic Preaching Is *Not*

I have listened to the preaching of many men who aspire to be prophetic preachers, but who fall far short of their goal. Typically they have a scowl on their faces throughout most of their message, and they shout from the beginning of their sermon to its end. Their message is disorganized, it has no clear theme, and it contains few illustrations. Yet, these men fancy themselves to be prophetic preachers. They imagine that they've preached a good sermon simply because they shouted the whole way through it.

What Prophetic Preaching *Is*

Prophetic preaching requires all of the same steps of preparation as does conversational preaching. Good prophetic speakers prepare meticulously. Their message has a clear theme and is well organized. They know exactly where they want to take their hearers. And they generously fill their message with illustrations and anecdotes.

Prophetic preaching differs from conversational preaching primarily in (1) the amount of prayer that has gone into the preparation and (2) in the manner of *delivery.*

True prophetic speakers depend heavily upon the enabling power of God. Leonard Ravenhill would typically pray every night for three to four hours for at least an entire week before preaching at a conference. So if you desire to become a prophetic preacher, first become a man of prayer. Fall on your face before God and seek His guidance and enabling power for your preaching.

Prophetic preachers also usually speak with a greater sense of urgency and with more intensity than would be found in a normal conversation. They shout at times. However, they don't just shout from beginning to end. They, too, use modulation— varying the volume and intensity of their voices.

If you feel called to be a prophetic preacher, I encourage you to first master the art of conversational preaching and all of the fundamentals of public speaking. Once you excel in those, then you can move on to the prophetic style of preaching.

Actually, good prophetic speakers typically begin their sermon in a conversational tone and slowly work up to a more intense level as the sermon proceeds. I know that's what Leonard Ravenhill did. And often he reached a peak of intensity and volume several times throughout a sermon, but then would go back to a conversational tone for awhile. He then built up to another peak and again flowed back.

Earlier in this book, I spoke about the need to be yourself when preaching. Men who truly are called to be prophetic speakers *are* themselves when preaching. They don't suddenly take on a new persona. Leonard Ravenhill was the same person whether he was in the pulpit or not. To be sure, he spoke in a more gentle manner in ordinary conversation, and he did not raise his voice as loudly. But he was the same man with the same intensity.

Pitfalls to Recognize

When I was in law school, the professor who taught us courtroom speaking once told us: "When you're talking to the jury and the law is on the side of your client, then you pound the *law*. On the other hand, if the letter of the law goes against your client's situation, but you have unusual facts that might make the jury sympathize with your client, then you pound the *facts*. And what if both the law and facts go against your client? Well then you pound the *table*!"

There's a lot of truth in what the professor said. Lawyers have become adept at pounding the table to convince juries to arrive at verdicts that are not in accord with the truth. That's one of the reasons why I chose not to practice courtroom law.

But effective prophetic preachers can sometimes be no better than lawyers. Some men have exceptional skills at dramatic preaching, but they use their gifts to persuade their listeners to believe things that aren't true. They use a theatrical voice and emotional intensity to pass off false teachings and to cover up poor logic in their arguments. Effective prophetic preachers have the power to sway their listeners to truth or to error. They can be used powerfully by God, or they can end up being a stumbling block.

So if prophetic preaching is your gift and ministry, use it humbly with complete spiritual honesty and integrity. Make certain that you're truly preaching from the empowerment of the Holy Spirit.

Discussion Questions

1. What is meant by the term "prophetic preaching"?

2. What are some of the goals of prophetic preaching?

3. What are some of the mistakes often made by men who aspire to be prophetic preachers?

Exercise

Instructor: Have each student prepare and deliver a 5-minute prophetic message on one of the following topics (or another topic of their choice):

(1) materialism   (2) gossip   (3) loving your enemy

27

Listeners' Pet Peeves

For the past several months, I've had an interesting time asking people to tell me what their pet peeves are when listening to preachers. The reason I did this survey is that very few of our listeners ever give us negative feedback about our preaching. They don't want to discourage us or hurt our feelings. So, we rarely know what it is that people like or don't like about our preaching. That's why I decided just to go out and start asking people for feedback.

Whether you're someone who preaches regularly or only occasionally, here's some feedback that your listeners would like to tell you but probably never will.

The No. 1 Peeve

The complaint that people voiced to me most often was a speaker who *rambles*. He doesn't have a clear theme or goal, and he frequently repeats himself. His listeners have no idea where he's headed—and he probably doesn't either. He goes on and on, merely to fill up the allotted time. The cause of this problem is lack of preparation.

No. 2: Lack of Eye Contact

The peeve I heard second most often was lack of eye contact. Although this is an issue of delivery, the problem also is usually caused by lack of preparation. When a speaker makes little eye contact with his audience, it's normally because he is ill-prepared and his face is buried in his notes. He has probably written out a complete manuscript of his entire message, or at least a very detailed outline of it. He's not speaking extemporaneously.

A second problem concerning eye contact is fairly unique to conservative Anabaptist churches. In the early church, men and women sat on different sides of their meeting place. In fact, this was the practice in most churches up until the 18th century or so. However, today this practice has disappeared nearly everywhere except in the conservative Anabaptist churches.

I've often noticed that many speakers in our churches look only at the brothers, who usually are seated on the speaker's left. I feel quite certain that the reason for this is simply embarrassment and self-consciousness. The speaker doesn't mean to slight the sisters. Nevertheless, this is a pet peeve of many of our sisters—and I don't blame them in the least. It's good to have a modest regard for sisters, but being afraid to look at them when speaking is carrying modesty too far.

I've sometimes been tempted to bring to church one of those electric highway signs that has a blinking arrow, telling traffic to move over to a different lane. I would point the arrow to the sisters' side of the church. And then when a speaker looks only at the brothers, I would turn it on to remind him to look at the sisters as well.

No. 3: Speaking in a Monotone

Closely behind peeves one and two is speaking in a monotone. Few of us speak in a monotone in normal conversation. Rather, our volume rises and falls. Our voice inflection frequently changes. In contrast, when someone preaches in a monotone, listeners have to fight to keep from falling asleep. So always speak with life and animation!

Not much better than preaching in a monotone is preaching in a singsong fashion. My dictionary defines *singsong* as: "a monotonous rhythmical cadence, tone, or sound." Unlike the monotone speaker, the singsong speaker does vary his cadence and tone, but it's in a dull, repetitive pattern. It's hardly the tone to deliver something as precious as the message of the gospel.

Other Complaints Produced by Poor Preparation

The following pet peeves are not presented in any particular order, but I've grouped them together because they're all a result of poor preparation:

Reading lots of verses from all over the Bible. As I've said, this is the lazy man's way of preaching: just massing together a bunch of Scriptures with little exposition.

Apologizing at the beginning of a message. Some speakers apologize at the beginning of their message. For example, they might apologize for their notes not being organized or for not researching out their topic as they should have. Or they might apologize for the topic of their message.

What a terrible way to start a sermon! The introduction is supposed to whet your listeners appetite for what will follow. When you apologize, it has just the opposite effect. You've just told your listeners that your message is probably not going to be very interesting or enlightening. What a letdown to the congregation!

Perhaps you're a person who often feels it necessary to apologize at the beginning of your sermons because your notes aren't organized or something like that. All right, go ahead and apologize. But I want to challenge you to be totally truthful about it. Instead of making up an excuse, why not be completely up front with your listeners and tell them:

"Even though I had plenty of time to prepare this message, I didn't consider it important enough to spend much time on. I view other things in life as more important. So I'm afraid you'll have to sit through a dull, disorganized sermon."

If you don't have the guts to honestly confess that truth to your hearers, then don't apologize. Instead, prepare properly, and you won't need to apologize.

Being wishy-washy about what you're saying. When speakers vacillate throughout their sermon, it generally means they chose the wrong topic. If you don't feel strong conviction about a certain subject, then preach about something else.

I realize that there may be instances in which it's good to present two opposing viewpoints. However, that should be the exception. Normally, you want to speak about something in which you strongly believe.

Peeves About Manner of Delivery

Various people also shared with me pet peeves that concern the manner of delivery:

Dramatic variations in volume. Some speakers love to reach a loud crescendo and then suddenly drop to a whisper. During the 1800s, that actually was considered the mark of a great orator. And no doubt there are some people and some churches who still like that style today. However, most listeners don't, as it was one of the complaints frequently voiced to me. That doesn't mean that if you're a prophetic preacher you can't occasionally shout. Just don't suddenly drop from a shout to a whisper.

Speakers with a combative spirit. Some speakers seem to start off with a chip on their shoulders. They speak to their listeners as though their listeners are their enemies. They talk down to the congregation as though the congregation were inferior. Such speakers often stereotype all men, or all wives, or all teenagers. Then they berate the entire group as though everyone in that group is automatically guilty of the same sins. This is not the spirit you should have when preaching.

Distracting Habits

I was a bit surprised that much of the feedback I received from listeners concerned distracting mannerisms. We speakers usually are not even aware that we're doing these things. Here are some examples mentioned to me: swaying back and forth like a pendulum, playing with one's suspenders, using repetitive gestures, jingling coins in one's pocket, and coughing or clearing one's throat into the mike.

Grooming Issues

Many listeners told me that it really bothers them when a speaker has an untidy appearance. So be sure to comb your hair and wear appropriate clothes. If you've gained a bit of weight over the years, don't wear one of your dress coats or shirts that is now too tight for you. One person told me it distracts her when she has to worry about whether the speaker's buttons are going to start popping off when he gestures!

Training Good Speakers

Obviously, we want to avoid the pet peeves I've just listed, because they detract from our messages. But many of our speakers do these very things. What is the answer? The answer is to give our brothers more training.

Exercises

a. **Instructor**: Have each student prepare a written list of the pet peeves they are sometimes personally guilty of.

b. **Instructor**: Have each student prepare a written list of five things *they* dislike in other speakers.

28

Growing Good Speakers

Good speakers aren't born. They're made. And a congregation can play an enormous role in growing a perpetual crop of good speakers. But just as a garden doesn't grow all on its own, good speakers can't be grown without planning and work on the part of a congregation.

Give Adequate Notice

The first step that your congregation can take to improve the quality of its preaching is to make certain that brothers receive adequate advance notice of their speaking assignments. Normally, brothers should be given their speaking notices at least a month in advance. Longer notice would be even better. The key to good speaking is thorough preparation. But speakers can't prepare adequately if they don't learn of their speaking assignments until the last moment.

Teach Public Speaking in Our Schools

If your church has a church school, make public speaking one of the required courses—particularly for your young men. Teach them all of the steps discussed in this book. Help them to learn how to speak extemporaneously with a conversational tone.

If the people in your congregation primarily homeschool, then encourage your parents to teach public speaking as part of their curriculum. Or perhaps your church could offer a separate public speaking course for all of your home-schoolers.

Provide Your Men with Training Materials

However, don't just depend on your church school or home-schools to do the needed training. Your church will need to do even more than that. "What more can our church do?" you may ask. The answer is that it can have an informal, ongoing training program.

To begin with, a church should provide every adult brother in the congregation with a book or manual that teaches the basics of public speaking. Your men are not going to just naturally know how to preach and teach without some sort of training materials. This book was written with that specific goal in mind. However, if there is another book or manual that you like better, by all means use it instead. The important thing is to get training materials into the hands of your men.

Have a Mentoring Program

Having a book that guides your men through the process of learning to speak effectively will be a huge help. But I recommend that you take it one step further. Have an ongoing mentoring program. Every devotional, every Sunday School lesson, and every sermon a brother delivers is an opportunity to advance in mastering the skill of public speaking. To that end, your church could assign one or more brothers who are adept at speaking to act as mentors or coaches for the other men.

What would such a mentor do? First of all, he would be available for others to consult with him about the message they're preparing. He could give them pointers on their choice of topic or theme. Perhaps he could even review their outlines in advance and help them firm them up.

Second, during church, this mentor or coach would listen to each speaker's message with an ear to giving both encouraging feedback and helpful advice on where and how the speaker could improve. Obviously, such a coach would need to be very tactful and encouraging. When Jesus gave evaluations to the seven churches in Revelation, He always began by commending them on something they were doing right—if at all possible. So the mentor should always find something for which he can commend the speakers.

Likewise, it probably would be wise if the mentor focused on only one weakness at a time. He wouldn't want to overwhelm a brother with a long list of shortcomings. It may be that the speaker first needs to learn to organize and logically develop his material. It may take a number of speaking assignments before he excels at this. Once he has mastered it, then he could move on to another point, such as speaking with modulation.

Such a mentoring program could be voluntary. If a speaker doesn't want to participate in it, then perhaps he could be excused from the program.

Sponsor Seminars and Bible Schools

On a wider scale, churches and church conferences can sponsor speaking seminars from time to time. Perhaps these could be weekend events led by experienced speakers. Such seminars could give the participants an opportunity to practice giving brief sermons, after which they might receive private evaluations of their messages.

Something similar could be done at youth Bible schools. The young students at these schools usually have reached the age at which they are ready to begin preaching devotionals in their churches. This means they're at the ideal age to receive needed training. Perhaps one of the courses in these Bible schools could be public speaking.

Be Prepared When You Travel

In many Anabaptist churches, it's customary that if another minister or designated speaker comes to visit family or friends, he's asked to preach that Sunday. Unfortunately, often he's caught unprepared. But as an ambassador of Christ, you should never be caught off guard. If you're going to be traveling and visiting one or more other churches on your trip, take with you one or two outlines of your better sermons. Then, if you're asked to preach, you'll be ready to deliver an interesting and powerful message.

Circulate Our Better Speakers

When a man spends hours and hours preparing an effective message, it's a shame for only one congregation to be blessed by it. Wouldn't it be a wise use of kingdom resources to exchange experienced speakers regularly between like-minded congregations? I'm referring, of course, to men who excel at speaking.

If our accomplished speakers could deliver each of their sermons at several different congregations over a period of a few months, this would make the most of their preparation time. In fact, it would multiply their effectiveness. Their home church, in turn, could be blessed by regularly hearing effective speakers from like-minded congregations.

Dependence on the Holy Spirit

Although most of this book has focused on the practical aspects of learning to preach effectively, I want to return to what I said near the beginning of the book about reliance on the Holy Spirit. Practical training is no substitute for seeking and relying upon the empowerment of the Spirit. When men and churches don't take preaching seriously, it invariably means that they aren't making preaching a subject of fervent prayer.

It means the men aren't asking God to help them become effective speakers that He can use in a powerful way.

At the same time, reliance on the Spirit in no way negates the need for preparation and training. God prepares the men He chooses to use.

Conclusion

The first preachers of the Gospel were men without any advanced education. However, they *had* received training from Jesus or His apostles. And they were a mighty army indeed!

There's nothing stopping our churches from producing such an army of powerful and effective preachers today. But to do so, our individual men must have a burning, prayerful desire to learn to be effective speakers. And we as congregations also must have the same fervent desire to train and assist our men in preaching.

All we need is prayer, desire and training. God will do the rest.

Discussion Questions

1. What are some of the ways that congregations and conferences can help to grow good speakers?

2. What is *your* congregation doing to grow effective speakers?

Bibliography

Baxter, Batsell Barrett, *Speaking for the Master*. Grand Rapids: Baker Book House, 1954.

Evans, William, *How to Prepare Sermons*. Chicago: Moody Press, 1964.

Perry, Lloyd M., *Biblical Preaching for Today's World*. Chicago: Moody Press, 1973.

Qualified to Be Ministers. New York: WTBTS of New York, 1967.

Willingham, Ronald L., *How to Speak So People Will Listen*. Waco: Word Books, 1968.

Zuck, Roy B., *Spiritual Power in Your Teaching*. Chicago: Moody Press, 1963.

Index

Special Pricing
for Congregations

Our desire is to see every man in our plain churches read *Plain Speaking: How to Preach and Teach Effectively*. To that end, we are making this book available to churches, schools, conferences, and individuals at the following special price when ordering 10 or more copies:

$3.00 per book
When ordering 10 or more books
Shipping is additional

Note: This price does not apply to distributors purchasing books for resale.

Scroll Publishing Co.
P. O. Box 122
Amberson, PA 17210
(717) 349-7033
Fax: (717) 349-7558